Whence and Whither

Also by Thomas Lynch

Fiction
Apparition & Late Fictions (2010)

Poetry
Skating with Heather Grace (1986)
Grimalkin and Other Poems (1994)
Still Life in Milford (1998)
Walking Papers (2010)
The Sin-Eater: A Breviary (2011)

Nonfiction
The Undertaking: Life Studies from the Dismal Trade (1997)
Bodies in Motion and at Rest: On Metaphor and Mortality (2000)
Booking Passage: We Irish and Americans (2005)
The Good Funeral with Thomas G. Long (2013)

Whence and Whither

On Lives and Living

Thomas Lynch (signature)

Thomas Lynch

Meri-Anne —
Well met again,
Blessings.

WJK WESTMINSTER
JOHN KNOX PRESS
LOUISVILLE · KENTUCKY

2019 Bear River

First edition
Published by Westminster John Knox Press
Louisville, Kentucky

19 20 21 22 23 24 25 26 27 28—10 9 8 7 6 5 4 3 2 1

Book design by Sharon Adams
Cover design by designpointinc.com

Library of Congress Cataloging-in-Publication Data
Names: Lynch, Thomas, 1948- author.
Title: Whence and whither : on lives and living / Thomas Lynch.
Description: Louisville, KY : Westminster John Knox Press, 2019. |
Identifiers: LCCN 2018036070 (print) | LCCN 2018037128 (ebook) | ISBN
   9781611649109 | ISBN 9780664264918 (pbk. : alk. paper)
Subjects: LCSH: Death--Religious aspects--Christianity--Miscellanea.
Classification: LCC BT825 (ebook) | LCC BT825 .L977 2019 (print) | DDC
   236/.1--dc23
LC record available at https://lccn.loc.gov/2018036070

This book is for Thomas G. Long

Contents

Preface

Therefore, since we are surrounded by such a great
cloud of witnesses, let us throw off everything that
hinders and the sin that so easily entangles. And let
us run with perseverance the race marked out for us.
Hebrews 12:1 NIV

When I found myself one recent year giving the Stanza
Poetry Festival Lecture on "The Body of Poetry," at
St Andrews University in Scotland, in the same buildings as
John Knox himself, "the thundering Scot," had preached his
Calvinism, it seemed as if I'd closed the loop between the
mysteries of faith and language, fate and happenstance that
have been among the chief intrigues of my work in words
since I first encountered them as a boy, learning the Latin
responses to the liturgy in the rectory of St. Columban's
parish in Birmingham, Michigan, where I grew up under
the religious tuition and moral sway of Fr. Thomas Kenny.
It was Fr. Kenny, may he rest in peace, who taught me the
Confetior, Kyrie, and Suscipiat and how to vest a priest for
early Mass, and when to ring the bell and light the wee char-
coal that kept a censer smoking so that the air around us
filled with the fragrance of heaven.

He had come from Salthill, north of Galway, out of a manse on Threadneedle Road, to attend Sacred Heart Seminary in Detroit with my father's uncle and the priest I'd be named for, Thomas Patrick Lynch. That sickly pilgrim, having survived the Spanish flu in his youth, and drawn to the priesthood by that dispensation, was sent out to Taos in the middle of the Great Depression in hopes that the high dry air of the Sangre de Cristos would lengthen the useful years of his ministry among the Pueblo Indians in their church, San Geronimo. He rode his circuit among the mission churches thereabouts and the Anglos and Hispanics who worshiped in them. He took sick and died after a couple years out West and was sent home to Jackson, Michigan, for burial.

It was there, in the embalming room of the Desnoyer Funeral Home, in late August of 1936, that his twelve-year-old nephew, who would in twelve more years become my father, watched the dead priest being lifted up and laid into the coffin his brother, my grandfather, bought on the day. It was then that the boy who'd become my father decided, having witnessed this thing, that he'd be an undertaker when he grew up.

"Why?" we would unfailingly ask him, whenever our father told us this story, "why didn't you want to become a priest?" After all, the priest was outfitted in liturgical vestments, green chasuble and stole, a linen alb, while the morticians on the day had only their starched white shirts well sweated through, striped formal trousers, black oxford shoes. Not one for metaphor or accoutrements, my father would always answer, "The priest was dead."

They are all dead now, the men and women who brought me into being—parents and grandparents, aunts and uncles, most all of them gone with the priests and nuns and undertakers of my father's generation—leaving only their stories and poems, the tunes they hummed, and what we remember of them. They all occupy their various perches in an ever more crowded, sometimes clamorous cloud of witnesses.

How did you come to be the one you are? is the question I've asked young writers to consider as an organizing query for the meditations that will become, if the spirits move, the poems and essays and stories they make out of the poems and essays and stories that came before. Look for the watersheds, the moments upon which everything seems to depend—the shape of the journey, the way home, the turn in the road from which vantage we see where we have come from and where we are bound, the whence and whither of our personal histories, the race we were born to run—those pools of happenstance out of which arise the life and times that bear our name and face, our being in the world.

That moment in the funeral parlor in Jackson, Michigan, more than a decade before I came to be—a moment of beholding an otherwise unremarkable task by a boy unschooled in the business of corpses—nonetheless shaped my father, my family, our futures; shaped me in ways that I recognize continue to reverberate through the still unfolding narrative. The nameless functionaries tending to the corpse of a dead priest whose name lives on now in me and my eldest son and his eldest son, each of us beset by questions about the mysteries, religious and existential, to wit: How did we come to be? Where are we bound when we die? Does the abyss on either edge of our linear history include us being in it? Are those boundaries of a somethingness or nothingness? What does it all *mean?*

Surely the dead cleric and the nameless mortuary sorts were beset by the same inquiries. Surely every human who ever was or is or will be will wrestle with these mysteries: the beauty of our being, the desolation of our ceasing to be. And when I look in the rearview mirror of my life, I see a procession of the reverend clergy and undertakers, men and women who kept the gates between the life we live and the lives we live in hope of—the heavens and hereafters we are always guessing at or getting little glimpses of. These edges and beyonds are where our cloud of witnesses abides, like the gallery in the courthouse balcony in that old film of *To Kill a Mockingbird*, where Scout and her brother look through the rail at their father pleading the hopeless case of an innocent in an all-too-often evil world.

So on my list of thanks are all the clergy and undertakers, ministers and morticians, poets and priests with whom I've spent the most of my time and attention through the years, rummaging through their poems and homilies for a clue, a cipher, a key to the meaning of it all; listening for something at graveside, fireside, bedside, in dark times and daylight, that made sense of our predicament. We live. We die. What's next?

The cahoots of the reverend clergy, Presbyterians in particular, brought this book into being. And I am grateful to them.

In the springs of 2014 and 2015, the theologian Thomas G. Long and I were shuttled around the state of New York to hold forth to ministers, medicos, and funeral directors on our coauthored book, *The Good Funeral: Death, Grief, and the Community of Care*. That book had been launched the year before at the 2013 National Funeral Directors Convention in Austin, Texas, where Dr. Long and I were invited to give the keynote address.

Our indenture to the New York State Funeral Directors Association took us to Columbia and Hofstra, Rensselaer Polytechnic Institute in Troy, thence to Syracuse and Albany, Buffalo and Rochester. We spent hours in cushy sedans crossing the interstates in the company of mortuary sorts who had, in league with their state association, organized the tour.

It was during one of those road trips that Reverend Long

took a call from Dr. Theodore Wardlaw, president of Austin Presbyterian Theological Seminary. It was that chat, I
suppose, that led to the letter I received some weeks later
from President Wardlaw inviting me to give the Thomas
White Currie Lectures in February 2016, which form the
gathering impulse for this book. The editor of our book,
The Good Funeral, David Dobson at Westminster John Knox
Press, got word to me that they would be happy to consider publishing those lectures and so the book you hold
was brought into being by Calvinists—teachers, preachers,
pastors and professors, homilists and scriveners who trusted
a devoutly lapsed but curious Catholic to hold forth in pulpit and print on subjects he owes his interest in to those of
bigger faith and better angels. I'm grateful for their benign
contrivance.

I am likewise grateful to Dean Jan Love of the Candler
School of Theology at Emory University in Atlanta and to
Alonzo McDonald, who funds the McDonald Chair with
that department. It is a cushy sinecure and allowed me to
read and write and team teach a course with Thomas Long
on the intersection of poetry, fiction, and homiletics in the
late winter of 2013. This was an obituary-class side hustle,
and like the years I spent teaching with Wayne State University's Mortuary Science Department and the decade I
spent with the Graduate Program in Creative Writing at
the University of Michigan, only the forbearance of my students allowed for the masquerade.

What I mean to say is that I've been allowed to play in
the deeper end of the pool than my schooling or counter-
feit erudition entitled me. I've been asked to read poems
or talk last things, the life of faith, and medical ethics, and
any number of other subjects, in venues around the English-
speaking world, from Adelaide to Edinburgh, Dublin to
Detroit, London, Ledbury, Los Angeles, and Winnipeg.

I've given lectures named for genuine professors, at uni-
versities of world renown, in churches and church basements,

institutes and galleries, libraries and bars—wherever I could get a crowd to outnumber me.

Some jobs I took because the pay was too good to pass up, others because it would read well in my obituary and maybe bedevil my siblings with envy in the end, others because a friend or mentor said I ought to, so I did.

But in the age of Trump such pretenses of competence are dangerous, and while a funeral director who writes poems is more like a proctologist with a sideline in root canal, confession is nonetheless good for the soul, as good for the cop who sings opera as the business mogul who pretends to public service.

So this is my confession, then. I do not know: I am agnostic on the whence and whither questions. Some days it all seems obvious to me—the loving creator, the gifts of grace, the everlasting light. Other days it seems we are entirely alone; brute nature is in charge, the end's the end. I do not know.

In addition to the aforementioned lectures, the pieces assembled here are from odds and ends from the hither and yon of those workaday endeavors. BBC Radio essays, a play commissioned by a community theater troupe in the west of Ireland but taken on by a community theater group in Northern Michigan, a story that needed a book to be in, and some poems the making of which bred longer meditations and narratives: four genres in search of God only knows.

I'm grateful to Kate McAll and Kate Bland who have commissioned and recorded some portions of these for broadcast on the BBC Radio, to the editors of journals and magazines in which some of these first appeared, including the *Journal for Preachers*, the *Christian Century*, *Commonweal*, *Poetry*, *Ploughshares*, *Conjunctions*, and others. I am likewise grateful for permissions to use poems or parts of poems, copyrighted by different publishers, that have instructed me over the years, a list of which licenses appears as an appendix to this text.

It would be remiss of me not to acknowledge my permanent thanks to Corrine D'Agostino and Emily Meier, bookish women and writers in their own rights, whose careful reading of and unstinting commentaries on this text have been essential to the work presented here. Both have been, each in her especial way, indispensable companions to this endeavor.

Finally, I am grateful to my earthbound cloud of witnesses —men and women of a fellowship notable for fearless and searching moral inventory, anonymity, salvage, and thanks, who insist that "the spiritual life is not a theory; we must live it." The reliable, often hard-won testimonies of these fellow pilgrims have been my good orderly directions for going thirty years.

TL
Milford
Mullett Lake
Moveen West
2018

Chapter One

Every Cradle Asks Us "Whence?"

This is the beginning.
Almost anything can happen.
This is where you find
the creation of light, a fish wriggling onto land,
the first word of Paradise Lost *on an empty page.*
Think of an egg, the letter A,
a woman ironing on a bare stage
as the heavy curtain rises.
This is the very beginning.
The first-person narrator introduces himself,
tells us about his lineage.
The mezzo-soprano stands in the wings.
Here the climbers are studying a map
or pulling on their long woolen socks.
This is early on, years before the Ark, dawn.
The profile of an animal is being smeared
on the wall of a cave,
and you have not yet learned to crawl.
This is the opening, the gambit,
a pawn moving forward an inch.
This is your first night with her,
your first night without her.

This is the first part
where the wheels begin to turn,
where the elevator begins its ascent,
before the doors lurch apart.[1]

These lines are from the opening of Billy Collins's poem "Aristotle," named for the Greek who believed that a "whole is that which has a beginning, a middle and an end." The structure of the journeys and stories, flights and lives—from nestling to fledgling to fully aloft, the narrative arc of rise and round and eventual fall, the sense that we all sometimes have of the structure of time and life, our own lives and times, that organize themselves into a starting point, a middle, and an end. If not entirely linear, it suggests a point at the beginning of a line that may do circles and loops but will eventually resolve itself into a final point sometime in the perilous, possible future.

And it strikes me as a kind of blessing on the setting forth that I sense myself making here this first week of February, this Groundhog Day, still shallow into the new year, wondering whether we'll see our shadows, or whether, as I've come to expect, we'll have six more weeks of winter, maybe a blizzard for St. Patrick's Day.

Last month for me, the yearly new beginning of January, was all embarkation and aubade, more lark than nightingale as birders say, winding out the daily increasing light that solstice and the festivals of light and the good Lord promise us. January hauls us into the prospect that we can, though old, begin again, though young, begin again, with new resolve to rid ourselves of our errant ways, our beer bellies, our tendencies to burn the bridges ahead and behind us.

January for me is all circumcision and epiphany—new resolve and sudden clarity.

Named for that two-faced, double-gazing god of beginnings and transitions, of doorways and gates, Janus bids us, as we consider where we are going, to have a look back on where we've been, how we got into the moment we're in, and how we came to be the ones we are.

Think of an egg, the letter *A*,
a woman ironing on a bare stage
as the heavy curtain rises.
This is the very beginning.
The first-person narrator introduces himself,
tells us about his lineage.

I am often introduced as a funeral director and a poet—this is, in the parlance of churchy sorts, a mixed blessing. I've a friend, a young Lutheran pastor, who has written a book on the subject of whiskey. Seems to me something better suited to Scots and Irish and bootlegger sorts. And while oddity and celebrity are near enough cousins that the former often passes for the latter, still, as my wife, Mary, is fond of reminding me, neither poets nor undertakers, sonnets nor obsequies are on most folks' lists of favorite things. Mine are not the "raindrops on roses and whiskers on kittens" sorts of interests, neither "bright copper kettles" nor "warm woolen mittens." Rather, my darling reminds me, an undertaker/poet is the occupational equivalent of a cop who sings opera, or, as is sometimes said about a disappointing blind date, "he was not exactly handsome but had a lousy personality."

Like Caesar said of Gaul, and Aristotle of the whole of things, my life is divided into three parts. The adventure in all ways seems if not Trinitarian, then triadic. Not only by beginning, a middle and an end, but by enterprise and endeavor, and by habitation.

I've three places I call home—in Milford, next to the funeral home; on Mullett Lake, in Northern Michigan; and in Moveen, in West Clare, Ireland, where I inherited the home my great-grandfather, another Tom Lynch, left more than a century ago to seek his fortune in America.

I spend a portion on the road, going from station to station, holding forth on a variety of topics, literary and mortuary. It is the portion that brings me here, and part of a larger mystery to me, to wit, why would anyone want to hear what I have to say about anything?

I have not studied or prepared for holding forth. I am not a preacher or lecturer by training or temperament. As a writer I speak mostly to myself in voices I make up out of thin air, maintaining only the slightest of hopes that someone will want to hear what my characters have to say. I will forever be an internationally unknown poet, a voice unheard on several continents, notable only to that relentless voice in me that says, "write on!" in the mantra of my feckless generation. And the voice's grim sibling who always whispers, "or else."

But all of your callings, I presume, are to preach and teach and to a priesthood of the holy, the voices you heard, like those heard by the apostles, "come follow me," or words to that effect.

Or maybe what you heard was silence. *Silent beyond silence listened for*, as Seamus Heaney called the loss of his dead mother's voice.

In response to which vocation, most of you will have taken a course called homiletics, in which you were encouraged toward hermeneutics and exegesis and the deeper reading of the sacred texts. And part of that course may have had something to do with how to hold them forth, to launch the words you write into the air where they make their way into the minds of others by the hearing of them. Holding them forth, giving them out, proclaiming the gospel, the good word, good news, in front of all these people.

The closest I ever came to such training came with the invitation in high school from one of the Christian Brothers, Brother Nash, to audition for the lead role in the Christmas play that he was planning on staging that year. He said he thought I'd have what it would take—to bring the character to life and project the character to the back of the gymnasium. I should show up that day after school when the drama club, of which he was the head, was inviting some fellows from our school and some young women from Marian High School next door (we Catholics kept the sexes separate but accessible through puberty and beyond) who would be auditioning for the lesser roles. I imagined myself being the baby Jesus or the blessed virgin—which indeed I was—or possibly St. Joseph, that poor cuckolded fellow. I could see myself in any of those principal roles, away in the manger, no room in the inn. But when I showed up for the auditions it turned out that Brother Nash wanted me to try out for Santa Claus, the first of my lines being "Ho, Ho, Ho!" It maybe goes without saying I got the part. I've been holding forth ever since to anyone in earshot.

I spend a fair portion of my portion on the road in Ireland, in Moveen, in the ancestral home of my paternal lineage— the hovel and habitat on the West Clare Peninsula from whence my great-grandfather and namesake, Tom Lynch, came to settle himself in Jackson, Michigan, a century and a quarter ago. His own father, Pat, had come over before him and found the great walled penitentiary in Jackson to be a work in constant progress, with cellblock after cellblock being added to house the ever-rising population of scoundrels and scofflaws that Michigan is well known for. (It should be said that these were the days before the mass incarceration of poor brown and black people as an extension of Jim Crow laws and race-based slavery became commonplace.)

For unskilled Irish, the stonework and ironmongery required to detain our fellow humans was the perfect fit for our skill set, requiring upper body strength and brain boxes sufficient to follow directions. I inherited, by the grace of Whomever's in Charge Here, the small stone house in Clare along with its haggard offices, sheds, and stable yard because

I was the first one of my family to return, forty-six years ago this month, after getting a high number in the Nixon Draft Lottery and figuring that my lackluster college career would not be damaged by my taking some time for independent study in the country of my forebears.

I was aware that we had an Irish connection because my grandfather, dead more than fifty years now, had always appended to his grace before meals—the standard popish rendition—the directive to anyone in earshot who shared his table, "and don't forget your cousins, Tommy and Nora, on the banks of the River Shannon. Don't forget." Of course, my grandfather had never been to Ireland and wouldn't have known the River Shannon from the Rio Grande, or Tommy and Nora from Ozzie and Harriet who had just turned up on a thing called television in those days. But, he'd been instructed by his father, my namesake, the Jackson Prison man, to pray for his family who held to the home place and kept alive his hopes that he might someday return. He never did. Nor did his son or his grandson.

It was his great-grandson (who, like Tommy and Nora, he'd never met, dead eighteen years before I was born) who bore his hopes back to West Clare and into the doorway of the home he'd left some eighty years before, on the third of February, 1970. "Tom that left," said Nora Lynch as she considered the block of a boy I was in those days, standing in the middle of the kitchen, "and Tom that would come back." She was nothing if not good for the rare and memorable pronouncement. I spent four months with Tommy and Nora that first time, learning to milk cows, muck out manure, fetch water from an open well, understand the thick brogue of the West Clare rural sorts, and connect the dots between this primeval life and the life I knew in suburban Michigan.

Or maybe the divisions aren't the wherefore but the when. Maybe my life is divided into the past, the future, and the moment here, now gone, that gift, that present we're always trying to make sense of just as I'm trying to find out in these colloquies exactly what it is I'm doing here.

Or maybe it's the how and why, those much-neglected adverbials. How does it work? I'm often asked about the twelve-step program I've been walking in for twenty-seven years. "Just fine," I tell whoever asks. "Just fine." So faith, or works, or amazing grace—my place and time and life seem somehow upheld by a triad of undeserved gifts, godsends I call them, knowing that there's nothing I've done to earn these gifts. So the life of faith—certain as I sometimes am that Whomever is in Charge Here is doing the job for which we designate gods to keep getting done. Or the life of doubt—wherein I wonder as I often do if there's anything at all we ought really keep faith in, the entire idea of theodicy and the bet-hedging answers we assign to it. Or the life of hope, helpless but hopeful, that whatever is supposed to happen will in fact happen. A life I gain entrance to by that one article of faith I've come to believe in unambiguously, to wit: if there is a God, it is not me. That seems to work, in the first-person, present-tense sense of things: I am not God.

Still it is hard to know—person or place or tense or time, sure faith or certain doubts, devout or devoutly lapsed? Hard to know, but still worth the wonder.

"Listen to your life. See it for the fathomless mystery it is. In the boredom and pain of it, no less than in the excitement and gladness: touch, taste, smell your way to the holy and hidden heart of it, because in the last analysis all moments are key moments, and life itself is grace." So writes Frederick Buechner in *Now and Then: A Memoir of Vocation*.

And I take his directive to heart, which is to say, I've experienced the lovely and instructive schism between what Barbara Brown Taylor calls "belief and beholding," between the way of things which we were taught and the way of things we've come to know by living them.

In the beginning I was a boy, the second son of a good man and a good woman, long since gone now, who made

their family after World War II in the image and likeness
of the ones they had known. They met in the middle of
the Great Depression, both students of the fifth grade at
St. Francis de Sales, one of the dozens of nunnish parochial
schools that kept kids ghettoized by race and faith. By the
time they graduated from high school, the world was at war
and they were a couple having danced to Glenn Miller and
Tommy Dorsey tunes under the stars at the Walled Lake
Pavilion. Before Christmas of 1942, he'd joined the Marine
Corps, trained in Southern California, and boarded a boat
bound for Melbourne, Australia, his letters home and hers
following him through the island-hopping war in the South
Pacific. They courted by proxy and Victory Mail for the next
three years, and when he came home from China in January
1946, they planned their wedding for that coming June.

    I grew up in the orthodoxy of Irish Catholicism—a com-
bination of tribal and religious doctrines best articulated in
the pages of Fr. McGuire's *The New Baltimore Catechism No.
2, Official Revised Edition* published by Benziger Brothers,
Inc., first published in 1941, and republished as needed for
the next twenty years. Its dictates and dogma got me from
birth until puberty, from original sin to the way of salvation. And in sacramental terms from baptism through con-
firmation, I'd been laved, absolved, fed, and enlisted into
the army of God on earth. Left only were the choices about
holy matrimony or holy orders and extreme unction, a thing
now called the anointing of the sick and which I myself have
had, in advance of some open-heart surgery five years ago,
to replace a stenotic aortic valve with a pig valve—blessings
be upon the pig—which restored me to a more inspired life.

    In actual fact, and here I digress, when I was told by my
primary care physician in consultation with the cardiologist
who had detected this troublesome murmur in my heart,
which signifies a valve job will be needed, and the cardiac
surgeon—God be with his hands—who would be cutting
through my sternum and into my heart; when I was told that

I would require, and fairly soon, this remedial intervention by the bloody high priests of modern medicine, the thing I asked was, "Don't I have some say in all of this? Have I any choices here at all?" Oh yes, the kindly medico told me, you can choose a cow valve or a pig, thinking there'd be some comfort in that. A cow, I told them, without hesitation, a Friesian cow now that I think of it. I've had good times pulling calves out of many a black-and-white bovine in the sheds where such things happen in Moveen. It's a bloody business, fraught with miracles.

In point of fact, when I awoke from the seven-hour savagery they'd done to me, the first thing I asked him was about the cow. In my delirium, medically induced, I'd been dreaming of plump udders and cheeseburgers. We gave you a pig valve, the doctor said. We thought it suited you.

I inherited the stenotic valve, so the doctors tell me, from my forefathers, all of whom died of broken hearts, infarctions, occlusions, emboli. My father's father, Edward Lynch, was a slight and balding man I always remember huffing and puffing, his lower jaw pushed out as if to scoop the air into his mouth. He died before the miraculous pig valves and cow valves could be cobbled into place, replacing the thickening flaps of his dysfunctional valve. He was sixty-three. I dressed his body with my brother Dan, placed him in a brown metal casket, which I helped to carry to his grave. My father died of a congested heart that failed while he was showering with his woman friend in southern Florida in mid-February twenty-four years ago. He was sixty-seven.

This writing began to take some real shape in November, a few years back, between the feasts of All Hallows and All Souls and the later and more secular observance of Thanksgiving—a varying if not movable feast that settles itself on the fourth Thursday of the balding penultimate month in the Roman Calendar.

Though I'd gotten the invitation to deliver the lectures

that sprang from this writing in early April, I kept putting off the eventual work in words, hoping that these lectures would find their way into being by some other method than pitiful scratchings on the blank page or typing into the blank screen and waking to revise, revise, and revise some more. Maybe the amalgam of genius and inspiration that has never, in my experience, produced a stanza or a paragraph worthy of publication—maybe that would save me from the torment of having to lay the words down, one after the other after the other in accordance with the scribes of the Old Testament, or the scriveners of the new one. It is true for poets and essayists, maybe it is so for exegetes and preachers, we wait until the deadline is upon us before bestirring ourselves into the actual doing of it.

I remember good Henry Stenner, the Presbyterian minister in Milford, Michigan, more than forty years ago, now.

How is it we never feel the time going? It was turn of the twentieth century Calvinists and Congregationalists who left the white clapboard church they shared on the south side of the river in my hometown of Milford, Michigan, to build this mighty fortress to the glory of God on the southeast corner of Liberty Boulevard at Main Street in Milford, during the gilded age more than a century ago—a red brick and mortar edifice to which they would later add classrooms, a chapel, a fellowship hall, and the basement offices of the preacher, the light in which, the years that Henry occupied the pulpit there, burned late into the Saturday night and early Sunday mornings as Reverend Stenner prepared his weekly homily. His years in that pulpit were coincident with the most steadfast and stumbling of my latter drinking days, and I'd often find myself driving home on Saturday night, down Main Street to Liberty then turning east to see the shadow of the churchman at his labors in the church basement, trying to get right what it was he should say to the blessed and elect who would fill his pews on the morrow.

Often I'd be tailed home by one of the local gendarmerie, who, knowing my habits, would follow me safely home and into the house rather than clapping me into leg irons and hauling me off to the pokey.

Having finished all but one of the year's gainful labors in October, I marked the holy days with my grandchildren and bags of candy. They were lemurs, skeletons, snowmen, and my granddaughter was done up as Raggedy Ann, in an outfit her mother made from scratch, thereby breaking the cute-o-meter entirely. On the eve of Guy Fawkes, I drove down to the home of the Fighting Irish for one last indenture at Notre Dame where I'd been hired by the Institute for Church Life to hold forth to students and faculty of the Character Project, where I was told by its director that I was on the syllabus, on matters mortuary. Having done just that, I woke early on the first Thursday of November in the Morris Hotel, performed the short form duties of my toilet and hit the road from South Bend, in northwest Indiana, imagining the bonfires still smoldering in East Anglia, and how the disputes between popish and Protestant sorts are settled now on the football field and at the ballot box. I stopped at home in Milford, Michigan, in southeastern lower Michigan to pick up my aged giant dog, Bill, and made for the interstate that took me north to our headquarters at Lines End on the south point of Mullett Lake, a perch just south of the Straits of Mackinac and the bridge that links my state's two peninsulas. You can find these places on a map. Or Google them, as we do.

Lines End is what my youngest son, Sean, named the place. It's on the lake at the end of Temple Road, end of the line. And, as a man accustomed to word play, Sean likes the several possible meanings of the name.

It's five years now since I made the move from one side of the lake to the other. The mouth of Indian River, part of the inland waterway, separates Lines End from Grand View

Beach, named for the vantage it has into every corner, bay, and backwater of the lake, where my parents first fetched up fifty years ago and where their sons and daughters began buying up cottages on the lake and ruining the property values by their company and habits. I shared a nice house over there with a brother and a sister and their families, but as my children grew into adulthood, the pressure for our own separate digs combined with my hunger for quiet and remove eventuated in our move over here. We rebuilt an old cottage that was easing into dereliction and declared it our compound and gathering place, away from our usual labors and habitation next door to or near enough to the funeral home downstate that bears our family name and from which I am not retired, but not required.

Most off seasons I am mostly alone except for Bill, who doesn't much care which floor he spends most of most days nodding on. My wife comes for the grandchildren's birthdays, the Fourth of July, the odd weekend in fine weather. Otherwise she makes her headquarters downstate where her parents, now into their anecdotages, and siblings nearing retirement, and friends in various stages of ease, keep her busy. So up here, it's mostly Bill and me. I read and write, he sleeps, we eat and snore and now and then go out to piss and look around for eagles and loons and red foxes and black squirrels. I just turned the age my father was when he died. Bill will be ten in a couple months, well past the expectancy his breed is assigned on Wikipedia, where six to eight years is pretty much the range a dog of his size can be said to bide his time. I'll have a grave dug this month in the hinterland where the county's abandoned road easement was divided between my neighbor and the folks who built this place back in the middle of the last century, coincidentally in the year I was born. When folks told me to tear the place down and rebuild from scratch, I always said I liked the old bones of the place, the stone fireplace, the oldfangled kitchen, and thought they'd be good for the longish haul.

So we added a broad, spindly porch on the lakeside, looking due north, dormered out the attic for bedrooms upstairs, added a sunroom on the east side and screened porches up and down on the west and built-in bookcases wherever we could. We got new appliances and redid the hardwood floors. Bill likes to bark at boats going by. I like to sip coffee in the Adirondack chairs on the front porch, counting my blessings.

When the grandkids are here, we have four of them now, I take them fishing and do bonfires with s'mores and scary stories. When my wife is here, it can be very special. When it's Bill and me, I mostly read and write. He eats what I eat, goes where I go, lives a life of ease here, nearing his end. This morning I made him oatmeal and a cheesy omelet. Tomorrow I'll thaw some perch. Sunday it'll be lamb chops and boiled spuds.

Listen to your life, write on, or else. Surely there's some wisdom in all of that.

On a cold, rainy day in 1882, a man named Robert Ingersoll stood over the new grave of a child and spoke these words:

> They who stand with breaking hearts around this little grave, need have no fear. The larger and the nobler faith in all that is, and is to be, tells us that death, even at its worst, is only perfect rest. We know that through the common wants of life—the needs and duties of each hour—their grief will lessen day by day, until at last this grave will be to them a place of rest and peace—almost of joy. There is for them this consolation: The dead do not suffer. If they live again, their lives will surely be as good as ours. We have no fear. We are all children of the same mother, and the same fate awaits us all. We, too, have our religion, and it is this: Help for the living—Hope for the dead.[2]

Help for the living. Hope for the dead. If there is a briefer or better motto for what vocation, education, and meditation have summoned us to, as ministry and mission to our fellow humans, I'm not able to imagine it.

It comes very close to the directive my father always raised over the work we mortuary sorts make it our business to do, to wit: to serve the living by caring for the dead. It is as if we are all assigned the one endeavor, this brokering of peace between the living and the dead.

Perhaps Ingersoll's rhetoric seemed an incarnation—his words made flesh of the fist that we humans shake in the face of the God when the worst that can happen happens, as it does.

Especially at the deaths of innocents, theodicy gets the foot of doubt into the doorway of our theologies, our faith.

"What good in this?" I remember asking any god in earshot, while dressing the body of a dead baby or toddler. "Is this the toll then, for the glory of God?" I do not think I am alone in this.

It happened when I called to condole with the undertaker, Dan Honan, of Newtown, Connecticut, who took care of many of the slaughtered six-year-olds that awful month a few years back.

"Why wasn't God watching?" Tom Waits wails in his song "Georgia Lee" on the death of twelve-year-old Georgia Lee Moses, who was kidnapped, raped, and murdered in Santa Rosa, California, in the summer of 1997. "Why wasn't God listening?" "Why wasn't God there for Georgia Lee?" Or drowned Syrian refugees, or the collateral damage of a gun-sick culture? Why wasn't God there as he was for Lazarus and Jesus? It is Job's old query shared by the bereaved forever.

It is kin to the case made in the eleventh chapter of the Gospel of John, where Jesus deliberately tarries in Capernaum so that Lazarus will be dead beyond any quibble, dead with the stench of death on him, by the time Jesus shows up, tardy in Bethany, to call the dead man, putrefying in his winding sheet, from the tomb.

"This sickness will not end in death," Jesus tells his apostles. "No, it is for God's glory so that God's Son may be glorified through it."

"If you had been here, my brother would not have died," says Martha, speaking for the heartbroken down the ages (John 11:4, 21 NIV). This is Job's imbroglio: How can God be both all-good and all-powerful and let such sadnesses happen? It's the foot of theodicy's doubt insinuated in the door of faith.

If the risen Lazarus is a harbinger of the risen Christ, the former a preview of the latter, then ours is a faith that makes its claims on the emptiness of empty tombs, and the dead who yet appear alive.

If theologian Thomas Long is right, and ours is a culture and a creed peopled by those who have "lost their eschatological nerve, and vibrant faith in an afterlife,"[3] maybe it is because we've grown unfamiliar with last things, the sick and dying and the dead, the grave, the tomb, the fire or sea to which we consign the bodies of the dead which, like the sick and dying, we no longer see. Just as the aged, demented, sick, and dying are removed from the custody and care of their families, the dead are often quickly disappeared by industrialized cremation that has become the norm for body disposition in many communities and churches—the funereal equivalent of a wedding without the bride or baptism without the baby or Calvary without the cross, the spilt blood and sacrificial gore. Our celebrations of life have become vapid equivalents to Easter without an animate corpse, saying to everyone in earshot, do not be afraid. We settle for the idea of the thing while the thing itself is steadfastly avoided.

Maybe we could go the distance with our dead—intimates and family, friends and co-religionists, colleagues and congregants, dead saints, such as they might be, fellow pilgrims. Maybe the best work any of us will likely do will be done at the graveside or the crematory or the crypt. That is where our cases are made in the maw of human mortality and grief, not the idea of the thing, but the thing itself.

Like Ingersoll on that desolate morning, the occasions we are bold to rise to are the best and worst of times, the new life, true love, fresh grief that inform the baptisms and marriages, burials and cremations we are called to comment on, preside over, officiate for. The relentless cycle of Sundays and holy days, feasts and festivals that pepper the liturgical calendar, the sick calls and counseling and pastoral visits, the committee meetings, the civic and secular enterprises that pastors and preachers are bidden to or drawn in by— few present the chance to channel help for the living and hope for the dead as those places where the ante is inevitably upped, the stakes are raised, and the faithful and those of shaken faith are teetering at the brink, ready to go all in, open to a restoration of eschatological nerve.

How we come to be the ones we are seems a question worthy of our inspection. I was named after my father's uncle, who survived the Spanish flu in his boyhood and reasoned he was spared for a higher calling. He became a priest.

Resolve anew to go the distance with them, the living and the dead, to the edge of whatever abyss we leave the dead to, commending their beings to God, coaxing the living home in hope. And if the living will not go the distance, as they more and more are disinclined to do, then go the distance with the dead on your own, as the primary office of your calling—to see your saints to the edge of whatever is or isn't next. The opened ground, opened fire, the hope of heaven or the claims we make for eternal life. Accompany them with singing and with faith. It might embolden the timid, shaken family to do the same, to join in some of the work of witness and vigil, watching and praying, digging and lifting and doing their parts in these primary human duties.

Chapter Two

And Every Coffin, "Whither?"

This is the middle.
Things have had time to get complicated,
messy, really. Nothing is simple anymore.
Cities have sprouted up along the rivers
teeming with people at cross-purposes—
a million schemes, a million wild looks.
Disappointment unshoulders his knapsack
here and pitches his ragged tent.
This is the sticky part where the plot congeals,
where the action suddenly reverses
or swerves off in an outrageous direction.
Here the narrator devotes a long paragraph
to why Miriam does not want Edward's child.
Someone hides a letter under a pillow.
Here the aria rises to a pitch,
a song of betrayal, salted with revenge.
And the climbing party is stuck on a ledge
halfway up the mountain.
This is the bridge, the painful modulation.
This is the thick of things.
So much is crowded into the middle—
the guitars of Spain, piles of ripe avocados,

Russian uniforms, noisy parties,
lakeside kisses, arguments heard through a wall—
too much to name, too much to think about.[1]

Billy Collins gets the middle right—the way we are strung out, hung out on a limb, pushed as we are by the labor of our creation, pulled as we begin to sense, toward our beckoning ends, the full frontal truth of our humanity: We die. And it is in middle life, that longish stretch we pray we'll have, after our schooling and sunlit youths, that the darkening sense of death's pendency begins to instruct us, years before it comes into view.

The middle is where we begin to live as if we will die someday. It's a growing up, a coming to terms with this quiet little truth: to wit, we die. And the numbers are fairly convincing on this, hovering as they do around a hundred percent.

And then what? If every cradle asks us whence, surely every coffin makes us question, whither?

I had this theory as a younger man, based upon the observation, a vantage gained by making funeral arrangements with young parents and old widows, to wit, the young look forward and the old look back, counterbalancing prospects and nostalgia. In youth we keep thinking about the future, in our age we dream about the past. The thought of death makes us careful at one end and bold at the other. And it came to me that we might be able to reckon middle age by monitoring the distance and direction of our visions, whether looking forward or looking back. When we seem most equidistant in our gazing, no more driven toward the future or haunted by our past, living in the moment, the present tense, it may be the marker of our middle age. Balanced between the past and future like a tightrope walker halfway in the journey. And knowing the middle, we might see the end—like algebra or geometry, a calculation of *a* plus *b* arriving at *c*.

Thus if we sense this middle ground at 33, figure on a death before 70. A pilgrim grown road weary at 20 might finish her journey by 40, whereas, one still striving at 50 might see a century before the angel of death eases them into what is or isn't next.

It happened to me when I was 41 at the end of October, All Hallows Eve. We had buried my mother that morning in Holy Sepulchre Cemetery, all of us standing around the abyss, the open ground into which we had to leave her, dead of a cancer at 65, then came home, desolate, to pass out candy to the trick-or-treaters, the ghosts and goblins, pirates and princesses, that run up and down the street among the scattering, skittering leaves, playing out themes of fright and fantasy. And maybe this is middle age when we learn to balance ourselves between our fears and fantasies. Our hungers and feasts, our highs and lows, our loves and griefs.

> And the climbing party is stuck on a ledge
> halfway up the mountain.
> This is the bridge, the painful modulation.
> This is the thick of things.
> So much is crowded into the middle—[2]

I remember falling into bed that night beside the blessed body of my paramour who made a gift of such comforts as humans do when they offer themselves to one another. After which I sat up looking out the window considering the mysteries of the day, my mother's burial, my darling's gifts, as if on the edge of the twin abyss of death and desire, beauty and bereavement, love and grief. And suddenly it seemed I had middle aged. That painful modulation, I had crossed the bridge. No longer on my way to becoming. I simply was, who it was I am, now, making my way, if my measurements were true, according to my theory toward 82.

So much is crowded into the middle.

Most daunting among the sentences in the invitation to deliver the lectures that became the genesis for the book that you are holding now was the one that read, "All of the various lectures will be delivered from the pulpit of Shelton Chapel."

That one sent a shiver through me that has, I'd hazard, run through those of you whose call is the call to preach, to hold forth, to say how it seems after everything—the prayer and meditation, exegesis and study, histrionics and hermeneutics, reading and writing and praying some more—how it seems to you in front of all those people.

Unlike you, I don't do this in response to a great commission, to the intuition of the voice of God, or to the sense of calling you could no longer hush or dodge. I do this because I am asked to do it and hired to do it and paid to do it and have often times found in the random happenstance of meaningful work, gainful employment and unexpected invitations, that in rising to some occasion I come to what Wallace Stevens called in his poem, "Not Ideas About the Thing but the Thing Itself," a new knowledge of reality.

If I say yes, if I cast my lot and keep faith in Whomever is in Charge Here, no harm will come to me, I tell myself, and possibly some good will come of it as we are promised instead.

So, yes is the answer I'm inclined to give, especially when I am asked by my betters, as truth be told I almost always am. "Always swing up in a bar fight, boyo," my long-dead father used to say. "Never swing down."

For just such a reason, whenever the proprietor of our local Dairy Queen would contact me in advance of the annual opening of his emporium, in most years soon after the spring equinox, to write a poem for the occasion, and come and read it, I'd always say no, especially as the stipendium he mentioned was always a credit at the window with his high-school girls, for banana splits, and malted milks, and other wonders of the soft-serve world. It's not my strong suit, I told him, occasional verse. What's more, I'd lie, I'm lactose intolerant or on a strict diet, trying, if not to lose weight, then to get taller somehow. Still, I began to miss his phone calls as soon as they stopped coming. He got, it turns out, some barbershop quartet-ers who would sing in harmony for most of the morning of the day he opened. Of course, they ate four times as much as I did and bothered the teenaged girls in ways that today we would call a hostile work environment, but just the same it brought a little crowd out for opening day.

But when the Librarian of Congress, or the Franciscans, or the Center for the Ethnography of Everyday Life, or the Institute for Character tenders the invite, yes is what I say.

Very rarely do poets get asked, get tasked, or paid, to stand and deliver. I've never, for example, been called to please give some sponsoring agency "that sonnet by next Tuesday, we really have to have it!" I've been pestered for essays and stories and especially newspaper columns, mostly for something far from important.

I was in Lafayette, Louisiana, years ago in the brief indenture of the National Book Foundation, who had me on the short list for their book award. I was going to local high schools with the intent of inspiring the nascent writers among them to fall into habits that might assure another generation of poets and writers. There was a lovely young woman from the foundation whose job it was to get me around from place to place who took me to the crawfish festival in Breaux Bridge, Louisiana, an event that I confess changed my life—people listening to live Cajun, which is to say Acadian music, whilst guzzling local brew and chomping on crawfish all in an excess, which they claimed to be its own reward. I scoured their faces as any Calvinist would, for signs of sinfulness and its attendant guilts and, finding none, finding nothing but a joyousness at being, being alive, being out in the day that was in it, among others of their tribe and different but similar tribes, I thought I was walking in abundant grace, the ever-present grace of being. Nothing has diminished, in the years since then, near twenty now, that it was meant to change me, meant to show me the beatific vision Mr. Ives once experienced on 51st and Lexington in that beautiful wee jewel of a novel, *Mr. Ives' Christmas*, authored by the Cuban master, the late Oscar Hijuelos. His hero, Mr. Ives, a kind, sad man who worked in an ad agency on Lexington Avenue, gets stuck in an elevator on the way out of work. When he is finally released, he buys a Snickers bar from the lobby vendors and walks out on to the pavement only to find himself smitten by the beatific vision of the "goodness of creation." Haunted by Dickens and the ghost of Christmas Past, the one around which his son was murdered, filling to the brim the pool of sorrows that the protagonist carries inside him ever since, he is unprepared for the deep sense of the beauty of creation and his fellow man that informs the vision on Madison and 41st Streets later that afternoon:

> Then something else unusual happened: walking down the street toward the impossibly crowded avenue, and standing shoulder to shoulder amid a throng of shoppers on the corner, Ives was waiting for the light to change, when he blinked his eyes and, in a moment of pure clarity that he would always remember, began to feel euphoric, all the world's goodness, as it were, spinning around him.
>
> In one slip of a second, anything seemed possible—had the moon risen and started to sing, had pyramids appeared over the Chrysler building weeping, Ives would have been no more surprised.[3]

Such visions—Ives's Christmas vision in New York, my Mayday vision in Breaux Bridge—have in common the sense they imbue us with that a loving God is surely in charge. They serve as countervailing weight to the everyday visions of murders, mayhem, atrocity, and random, meaningless suffering that punctuate our daily news and entertainments.

The same night of that crawfish festival, this was May of 1998, I got a call from the editor of the op-ed page at the *New York Times*, wanting to know if I'd given any thought to the fact that new DNA science made it possible to find out if the remains of an unknown soldier from the war in Vietnam was actually one or the other of two of the most likely candidates, and the question on the table for the Secretary of Defense was whether knowing was better than not knowing when it came to the long buried and much honored dead.

I'd not given that any thought, I told them, but would be happy to do so and get back to them. Very well, the editor told me, but whatever thoughts you have, you should shape them into 750 words and have them to me by this time tomorrow. But I'm an artist, I thought to myself, an internationally unheard-of poet and a literary essayist, not some hack reporter. "Well," she said, "around here, done is better than good." "What would you be giving me," I asked her, thinking we should settle the question of dosh up front. "A million and a half readers," she told me, and I was hooked. Readers are like cocaine for writers, just as folks in the pews, listeners are, for preachers.

All of us want to be known by strangers, accountable for our thoughts and words. And we are hopeful that the more are indeed the merrier. Whereas for poets to be outnumbered is a great success, to be outnumbered by a dozen is worth writing home about; to be outnumbered by hundreds is obituary level in the way of accomplishments. "He presented to a standing room only audience of faculty, students, and the reverend clergy at Austin Presbyterian Theological Seminary," was the way I began to shape the sentence in the obituary file I keep back home, always open to emendation. It kept the fearsome text about the pulpit and the chapel at bay long enough to respond to the invitation, yes, yes, yes.

One of the gifts of the half century I've spent directing funerals—from the 1960s when I was first becoming sentient, to the Two Thousand and Teens when I did not retire but was no longer required to assist my sons and their associates in the day-to-day enterprise of getting the dead where they need to go and the living where they needed to be—one of the value-added blessings of that long indenture in the service of the living and the dead is that I've listened to give or take twenty-five thousand funeral sermons.

To be sure, not all of the bodies were brought into church, or preached over in a funeral parlor, though that was the done thing through most of my career. The schedule of the obsequies went something like this: the body would be removed from the place of death after I would get what we called the First Call—we had preprinted pads of First Call sheets beside every phone at the office and at home, which included the template of facts required to trigger our involvement. We lived in constant readiness and anticipation of the call that would come, in the middle of the day or night, the middle of dinner or cocktails, the middle of Christmas or trick or treat, dance class or at the orthodontist. Every possible intimacy could be interrupted by a first call. Every one.

"Someone better be dead," my beloved used to say, when the phone would ring in the middle of the night next to the smaller bed we shared in those days. The light on the nightstand would go on, I'd be fumbling for a pen that worked, trying to get the sleep out of my voice and some empathy into it. Name, Age, Place of Death, Next of Kin, Person Calling, Relationship to Deceased, Phone Number of Person Calling, Doctor's Name, Arrangement Appointment Time, some lines for Notes. These notes, miscellaneous and incidental to the vital stats, included such things as church affiliation and reverend clergy. I soon learned that if a local corpse was lapsed Catholic, say, or Methodist, devout Presbyterian or backslidden First Baptist, Pentecostal or non-observant Jew, I'd have some sense of the wheel that had already been invented to work the space between the living and the dead, and, indeed, between the dead and their final disposition. Italian Catholics wore black, churched Baptists wanted an altar call while they sang "In the Garden," the secularists liked poetry and eulogies, the Jews all went to the edge of the grave, threw dirt, sat Shiva, said Kaddish, and got back to work. Still, the elements of the First Call had much in common, the adverbials, the who, what, where, and whenness of mortality. Later the adverbs would be expanded into a narrative at the arrangement appointment when the family and I would meet to discuss not only what had happened, but what we were going to do about it.

Often this is where you come in. The observant and devout will have their pastor's number on speed dial, whereas the family that has let the ties that bind them to a particular congregation loosen or fray will hope there is some shred of remembrance or thread of connection on which to tether their call for help. Or maybe they ask their undertaker to arrange for someone to say a few words on the occasion. They are lost and need help to find their way.

No one brings their B game to a funeral sermon. From my place in the bleacher seats you're making some remarkable claims: to wit, all things work together for some good. Chance that on the parents of those school kids shot at Newtown a few Advents ago. There's a heavy helping of theodicy, a heavy lift. The feigned sympathies of politicos, the faux gravitas of the news crews, the fellow feeling of our friends and neighbors seems an entirely insufficient counterweight to the evil of six-year-olds shot in their school rooms. Or a toddler raped and murdered by a fiend, or another dead of the croup one Christmas Eve.

Some years ago I was asked to write a poem to accompany a newly produced orchestral suite and song cycle by Evan Chambers, a young composer from the University of Michigan who, after touring an old burial grounds in Jaffrey Center, New Hampshire, felt moved to music by the limestone markers that commemorated the lives buried below them.

Sometimes, to read the dulled etchings on the stones, Evan had to lie prostrate on the grave and propped on his elbows to examine the old texts close up. He took rubbings of some, made notes on some others, already the music taking shape in his ears, the joyous sense of creation coursing through his brainy regions, the cloud of witnesses humming to him as if the long-dead pilgrims gone to their dust and ash under the ground were making noise again, their voices coming alive in him. He ended up in a kind of creative frenzy from which only the sharing of those voices with a wider world would give him pause. He came away from the graveyard with a community of the dead and gone and a sense of calling to tell their stories. He could not get it done alone. There were many characters to choose from. I was given Isaac A. Spofford, a young boy, the son of a deacon. His tombstone over grave number 078 of Jaffrey Center's Old Burying Ground reads:

> Here is entered the remains of Isaac A. Spofford, son of Deacon Eleazar and Mrs. Mary Spofford, a brand plucked from the ashes of Rev. Laban Ainsworth's house, 13 February 1788, age 8.

A dead boy from a different century, another winter, another town.

The exegetes among you will be rummaging your brain boxes now because something in that headstone's citation echoes in your memory. That brand plucked from the ashes re-rings a bell that first sounded in your readings of the Old Testament, the book of Zechariah, chapter 3, which records the cleansing of the high priest, Joshua, a harbinger of Jesus, the Savior, the high priest of a newer testament, how he was purified by God's grace, from any taint of sin or corruption, because, we can infer, God clothes his priests and presbyters, his ministers and teachers, in the spotless white linens of innocence.

Here is Zechariah 3:2:

And the Lord said to Satan, "The Lord rebuke you, Satan! The Lord who has chosen Jerusalem rebuke you! Is this not a brand plucked from the fire?" (NKJV)

Possibly, the Methodists among you will hear, deep in your memory again, the story of little Johnny Wesley, whose father, like Robert Ingersoll's, was a churchman hounded by his co-religionists, in Epworth, a little northwest of Doncaster in North Lincolnshire in the United Kingdom, where, it is rumored, they set his house ablaze, when John Wesley was a five-and-a-half-year-old boy.

It's late on the night of the 9th of February in 1709, Samuel Wesley is the rector of the Epworth Parish and lives with his wife, Susannah, and their seven daughters and three sons in the rectory, which is suddenly ablaze. All but John make it out of the house and into the garden when the boy appears in the second-story nursery window. His father commends the boy to the Lord, but it is a pair of local men who form a kind of human ladder and rescue the boy from the fire. It is Susannah to whom we attribute the thanks, holding her boy in her embrace, "a brand plucked from the fire." Surely, they all believe, he was saved for a higher purpose; thus do we discern the will of God in the mercy and goodness of happenstance. Isaac A. Spofford's stone, however, assigns his death, his body plucked from the ashes of a house that burned to the ground, to God's will. You can read it in a pair of rhyming quatrains that follows the adverbials and gives the reader an unambiguous directive:

Oh say grim death
Why thus destroy
The parents' hopes
Their fondest joy

Cease man to ask
The hidden cause
God's will is done
Revere His laws

I assigned these grim and bitter sentiments to the only man in Jaffrey Center, New Hampshire, who would have been called upon to provide the first draft of memory, the local parson in whose house fire the boy had perished.

The Reverend Laban Ainsworth turns out, as the University of Google will instruct, to have been notable for the longest continuous ministry in American History, from his calling to Jaffrey in 1782, after serving briefly as a chaplain in the Revolutionary Army and preaching at his own graduation from Dartmouth College where some Jaffrey folks first heard his homiletic powers, until his death at age 100, on St. Patrick's Day in 1858—seventy-six years of ministry to the one crowd, generation after generation. Let me read you a brief summation of the man's life from www.jaffreyhistory.org, written by Albert Annett and Alice Lehtinen:

> Without detracting from the divinity that hedged a minister of the old days, Laban Ainsworth entered into the everyday life of his people. He bought and sold and bartered with them. He was an extensive owner of real estate. He cleared away forests, grubbed out stumps, fenced mountain pastures, loaned the fruits of his thrift to those less fortunate on real estate mortgages. He went hunting and fishing, shot foxes and bears. He belonged to the Masonic Fraternity and Liberty Society; he debated with the schoolmaster before the Washington Benevolent Society; he was superintendent of schools; he visited the sick and the well; he catechized the children, he knew the fathers and their children unto the third and fourth generations. He was fixed in his religious beliefs and yet was tolerant of the opinions of others. He advised in town meeting and no one's counsel carried

greater weight. He was a business man but the title of Parson came first. In the old sense, he was above all the shepherd of his flock. As he grew older, his people called him Father Ainsworth. Sometimes they called him priest, which to them bore the same meaning, but parson, not minister, was the accepted term of endearment and respect. He had a keen sense of humor and could bandy words or play harmless practical jokes with the best of them. He was addicted to the weed, that is, he was a prodigious chewer of tobacco, a social accomplishment that had its uses in the argumentative circle before the tavern fire, but, withal, he had a profound sense of the dignity of his office and was ceremonious to a degree unapproached in these latter days.[4]

And here is the poem I wrote for maestro Chambers's orchestral suite, to retell the story of Isaac A. Spofford, reposing in Jaffrey Center, lo, these couple hundred years.

OH SAY GRIM DEATH

No doubt the Reverend Ainsworth read from Job
Over the charred corpse of the deacon's boy
To wit: "Blessed be the name of the Lord"
Or some such comfortless dose of holy writ
That winter morning after the house fire
Put all the First Congregationalists
Of Jaffrey Center, New Hampshire
Out weeping and gnashing, out in the snow
While the manse at Main Street and Gilmore Pond Road
Blazed into the early Thursday morning.
God's will is done as often without warning
As with one. Either way, *Revere His laws*
Is cut into the child's monument
To rhyme with a previous sentiment:
Cease, Man, to ask the hidden cause. As if
The answers ever were forthcoming. So
Little's known of young *Isaac A. Spofford* –

His father, *Eleazar*, his mother, *Mary*,
His death on the *thirteenth of February*
In *Seventeen Hundred, Eighty-eight*.
A brand plucked from the ashes reads the stone
Of Rev. Laban Ainsworth's house; which frames
The sadness in the pastor's burning faith,
In God's vast purposes. As if the boy
Long buried here was killed to show how God
Makes all things work together toward some good.
And yet the stone's inquiry still haunts:
Oh Say, grim death why thus destroy
The parents' hopes, their fondest joy—
Or say, instead, grim death destroys us all
By mighty nature's witless, random laws
Whereby old churchmen, children, everything—
All true believers, all who disbelieve,
Come to their ashen ends and life goes on.[5]

I have found myself as, I will hazard, most of you have found yourselves, confounded by countervailing senses, each one as keenly felt as the other, each one as studied, each one as true—that we are children of a loving God and that we are entirely alone.

I cannot believe, as Ainsworth did, that Isaac Spofford's death was the will of God. Nor do I believe in the doctrine of original sin, not since the first of my children were born, never since the birth of my grandchildren. Their innocence, like grace, is manifest and evident. Some days, I behold, they need a change of diapers, sometimes total immersion is the thing. But baptism is more a naming and claiming than laving and purification, just as the common meal of Holy Communion is more the table and the talk than the body and blood.

I behold in my own life the grace of God, as well as the sense that we might be all alone. And that death gives us, against all odds, our first glimpse of what is or isn't next.

So I'm more moved to goodness by the case of Robert Ingersoll, that notorious disbeliever, who said, "I deny nothing, I believe nothing, I know nothing, I wait and hope."

I think his confession suits me. I wait and hope. I keep my eyes wide open for the signs that we occupy a life overseen by a loving God, a true parent, the one in charge of our creation, our living of life on life's terms and the good orderly direction toward the way back home. The rest is up for grabs, whether substitutionary atonement, the moral influence theory, redemptive suffering, the Trinity or Beatitudes, although it is hard not to believe in the Beatitudes, or as far as that goes, the Sermon on the Mount.

The man who has reformed me the most and ministered to me the most and offered me a dose of good orderly direction is Thomas G. Long. He's a Presbyter and Preacher, a Teacher and Priest, and one of the blessings in my life of late. As is often the case among bookish sorts, I knew his paragraphs before I knew his person, so when we were virtually introduced by a funeral director in North Carolina, Mark Higgins, we knew we'd eventually have to meet, which we did, in 1997 or 1998, while he was still teaching at Princeton Theological Seminary and I was on a book tour that took me east. He picked me up at the airport and took me to lunch and we have been friends and co-conspirators ever since. The interest we shared, some of you will know, is in funerals, last things, matters mortuary, and the whence and whither themes that bedevil, bedazzle, and beleaguer us all.

My brother Pat, a great man entirely, while serving as president of the Michigan Funeral Directors Association got it into his mind that he'd like to hire Reverend Long and me, as the only funeral director at that time to have a book reviewed in the *New York Times*, to go around the state to meet with clergy and mortuary workers and discuss their shared interest and influences on local funeral customs. This we did in the spring of 1999, traveling from Marquette in Michigan's Upper Peninsula to Traverse City and Saginaw, Grand Rapids and Detroit in southeastern lower Michigan, speaking to over 1,500 clergy and funeral directors. I like to think that trip around Michigan provided some fodder for his masterpiece of mortuary arts, *Accompany Them with Singing—The Christian Funeral*, which if you have not read, you must do if you plan to take up pastoral duties.

A few years later we conspired to write a book on this topic, a book for young mortuary sorts, young clergy persons and seminarians, to help frame the conversation the culture has been having for more than fifty years about the makings of The Good Funeral, which became the title of our co-authored book.

Among the many fine things that happened after meeting is that I was given, again through the intercession of Reverend Long, a cushy sinecure at the Candler School of Theology at Emory University. This job provided an apartment and generous stipendium for a spring semester at the university, where my only duty was to show up each Friday for a class Dr. Long called the Poetics of the Sermon. He is one of the world's great preachers, and so the teaching of preaching is something he has done for most of his ministry. No doubt many of you have read his books. And some of you will have heard him preach, as I have, giving thanks for the uplift and challenge and elucidation it unfailingly supplies.

I have the fondest memories of my time at Emory, that late winter into spring some years ago now, among the Methodists and Presbyterians, First Baptists and Episcopalians. Of course, I learned much more from them than they would have learned from me. All of my free time was spent in the apartment, working away at the long fiction, surely the only novel I'll ever attempt, which has and still vexes me. Progress not perfection, we always say, which applies to fictionists and preachers, or so it seems.

A few years back I was more than honored when I was

asked to write a poem for the Festschrift that was planned to honor Tom in his retirement. "All poets borrow," said T. S. Eliot; "great poets steal." Possibly the same is true of preachers and pastors and parsons and presbyters. So I chose as the title of the poem I would write, before I had written a line of it, "What Shall We Say," because I think it is the query that keeps the preacher up most Saturday nights, wondering what they're going to be saying on Sunday. And it is also the title of one of Tom's books, which addresses, as the subtitle promises, "Evil, Suffering and the Crisis of Faith."

So these are the deep end of the pool concerns we humans have, whether creatures of God or creators of God, wondered about and worried over, stayed up nights looking into the fire or the darkness or the abyss. What shall we say when we are called to rise to the occasion? What can we say that might offer some succor or comfort or peace in the teeth of the storm, the face of mortality, the terrible maw of the shit that happens?

Why is it, I guarantee you will be asked, Miriam doesn't want Edward's child? Or maybe she did but they found themselves unable to conceive, and it broke their hearts and resolves and led inevitably to the end of their marriage, or maybe they stayed together and adopted a child from Guatemala who ended up on drugs and died of a heroin overdose. What shall we say? What will you say? Help for the living? Hope for the dead? Cease man to ask the hidden cause, God's will is done? Revere his laws? I deny nothing, I believe nothing, I know nothing, we wait and hope?

What shall we say to the young widow, the old soldier, the newly unemployed, the abused child, battered spouse, wounded hero, minor poet, doubting Thomas, helpful Hannah, maiden aunt, drunk uncle, next door neighbor, gay teenager, perfect stranger—all of whom I guarantee will find their ways into your pews or office or parking lot or front yard or the long night of your soul—and in each of whom you will have to discern the child of God however hidden, because God is love and who abides in love abides in God and God in her.

All I can testify to are the times I knew that, if God is love, as John instructs us, then I've seen God and more than once. And not where I expected.

I've seen God in the county courthouse where my sister and her partner of twenty-five years stood in line with the other couples the culture and the church still thought of as "queer" for a license to marry and parent together and be nexts of kin. The belief, the magisterium of my church says they are "disordered" in some essential way, but what I behold is that God is love.

I saw God two Sunday nights ago in the basement of Transfiguration Church where I attend an AA meeting and where one of the recovering drunks like me said that something she'd heard at that table helped her to lay down the long resentment that threatened her sobriety. To the triumphalist, blessed and elect, she is a loser, a loner, a weak-willed addict, but if God is love, God shone from her, filled the room with grace, however undeserved, however abundant, that upheld us all. And I've seen God almost every day, when someone gets out of their Barcalounger on a cold evening, quits the *Law & Order* reruns and brushes their teeth and hair and comes to the funeral home to pay their respects to the dead grocer or grandmother or fellow pilgrim, though they cannot fix it or raise the dead or bring any more comfort than their being there. That is love and love is God is love.

And coming home those Saturday nights for years with a snoot on, seeing the lights in Henry Stenner's office burning the midnight oil over his morning's sermon, it seems like seeing Love again and Faith and Hope, which is why when they asked me to write a poem for Thomas Long's retirement, I had faith in the language and the lexicon as each of you will have to do in answer to the question, "What shall we say?"

I always begin with a dictionary. One with some notes on etymology. I looked up the meaning of the word "pulpit." It comes from the Latin, *pulpitum*, meaning "scaffold" or "catafalque." The sense one certainly has occupying the pulpit, feels like a scaffold meant for an execution. It feels like being too far out on a limb. It feels like we're alone in front of all these people. What shall we say?

I remember the first time I felt the power of words. I'd grown up knowing that poetry was whittled, sharpened speech, like a spear head or a knife able to cut and puncture. My first prayer—angel of God my guardian dear, to whom God's love commits me here—was a poem. Next door at the Methodists they were saying, now I lay me down to sleep and pray the Lord my soul to keep. Different rhyme, different meter, different words, same grim thought. My first pronouncements—twinkle, twinkle little star, how I wonder what you are—my first letters and lessons—abcdefg, hijklmnop—all poems, trochee, trochee, falling thus, grief and meter order us. But I was in high school, and after the great job I'd done as Santa Claus in the Christmas pageant, I thought I'd try out for the spring play. They were doing *The Glass Menagerie* by Tennessee Williams, which meant nothing to me. What I knew was that many of the Marian girls from next door would be working the production, and all I could think of was getting to know them better. I read the play, which begins, and ends, as you may remember, with Tom Wingfield, the play's narrator and the brother of Laura, who collects the glass figurines that give the drama its title, out on the fire escape speaking into the dark where the audience listens.

Yes, I have tricks in my pocket, I have things up my sleeve. But I am the opposite of a stage magician. He gives you illusion that has the appearance of truth. I give you truth in the pleasant disguise of illusion.

To begin with, I turn back time. I reverse it to that quaint period, the thirties, when the huge middle class of America was matriculating in a school for the blind. Their eyes had failed them or they had failed their eyes, and so they were having their fingers pressed forcibly down on the fiery Braille alphabet of a dissolving economy.

In Spain there was revolution. Here there was only shouting and confusion.

In Spain there was Guernica. Here there were disturbances of labour, sometimes pretty violent, in otherwise peaceful cities such as Chicago, Cleveland, Saint Louis. . . .

This is the social background of the play.

[MUSIC]

The play is memory.

Being a memory play, it is dimly lighted, it is sentimental, it is not realistic.

In memory everything seems to happen to music. That explains the fiddle in the wings.

I am the narrator of the play, and also a character in it. The other characters are my mother Amanda, my sister Laura and a gentleman caller who appears in the final scenes.

He is the most realistic character in the play, being an emissary from a world of reality that we were somehow set apart from. But since I have a poet's weakness for symbols, I am using this character also as a symbol; he is the long-delayed but always expected something that we live for. There is a fifth character in the play who doesn't appear except in this larger-than-life-size photograph over the mantel.

This is our father who left us a long time ago. He was a telephone man who fell in love with long distances; he gave up his job with the telephone company and skipped the light fantastic out of town. . . . The last we heard of him was a picture postcard from Mazatlan, on the Pacific coast of Mexico, containing a message of two words— "Hello - Good-bye!" and no address.

I think the rest of the play will explain itself.[6]

Many of you remember the play ends with Tom out on the fire escape again, ending as the play began with him speaking into the dark.

I didn't go to the moon, I went much further—for time is the longest distance between places. Not long after that I was fired for writing a poem on the lid of a shoebox.

I left Saint Louis. I descended the step of this fire escape for a last time and followed, from then on, in my father's footsteps, attempting to find in motion what was lost in space. I traveled around a great deal. The cities swept about me like dead leaves, leaves that were brightly colored but torn away from the branches. I would have stopped, but I was pursued by something.

It always came upon me unawares, taking me altogether by surprise. Perhaps it was a familiar bit of music. Perhaps it was only a piece of transparent glass. Perhaps I am walking along a street at night, in some strange city, before I have found companions. I pass the lighted window of a shop where perfume is sold. The window is filled with pieces of colored glass, tiny transparent bottles in delicate colors, like bits of a shattered rainbow.

Then all at once my sister touches my shoulder. I turn around and look into her eyes . . .

Oh, Laura, Laura, I tried to leave you behind me, but I am more faithful than I intended to be!

I reach for a cigarette, I cross the street, I run into the movies or a bar, I buy a drink, I speak to the nearest stranger—anything that can blow your candles out![7]

I didn't get the part. I worked in the wings, pulling curtains, moving scenery around. The part went to John Hildebrand, now a writer and professor in Wisconsin. But I remember how it made me weep, to hear him say these words out on that stage, alone, as if on a fire escape in St. Louis, or how this Tom or the frightened, doubting Thomas in each of you will crawl out on your limb every Sunday wondering what it is you're about to say.

After the dictionary I looked at the last page of a magazine, the *Christian Century*, where Lil Copan was writing about a painting I love of the Sermon on the Mount. I was off and running. I will end with the poem I wrote that day, a poem, like the panels of religious art I often admire in museums, divided, like my life and times, like my homes and habits, like the Father, the Son and Holy Ghost, like Aristotle said of wholes and they said of Gaul—into three parts, a triptych for Tom Long, from whom I'd steal the title, "What Shall We Say?"

WHAT SHALL WE SAY?

A triptych for Thomas G. Long:
teacher, preacher, presbyter

I
The etymology is perilous:
pulpit from *pulpitum*, meaning *scaffold*,
by which we come, at length, to *catafalque*—
those f's and a's, like tongue and grooved boards,
like rope enough to hang, or hoist, or let
a corpse down to its permanent repose.
One platform's raised; one frames a coffin's rest.
So, first the elocution, then the wake?
Like lamentations or the case of Job—
that vexing, god-awful, comfortless book.
And yet we rise to the occasion,
Sunday after Sunday after Sunday.
A bit of scripture, a psalm or poem,
something that happened in the week just past;
we try to weave them all together as
if to say a loving God's in charge.
As if we were certain of a loving God.
We see by faith. We live in hope. We love.
Or play the odds, as Pascal did. We fall.
Sometimes it all seems quite impossible.
And yet we rise again and walk the plank,
and sing into oblivion good news:
Unto God the glory, all praise, all thanks!
while nodding congregants loll in their pews.

II
Imagine Tom out on the fire escape,
between the world at large and inner life,
edging the proscenium, downstage right,
whilst curios and characters and shades

unveil themselves as dancing beauties do.
I have tricks in my pocket, things up my sleeve!
Upstage, sheer curtains rise, transparencies:
Truth in the pleasant guise of illusion.

Like John on Patmos, John the Harbinger—
voices crying out of the wilderness—
Make straight ye the Lord's way! quoth Isaiah.
Eschatology and Apocalypse:

Think Esmeralda in the cathedral,
Jim Hawkins in the riggings, chased by Hands
or Ishmael, just flotsam at the end,
alone, before God and all these people.

Or Montaigne in his tower library:
"the whole of Man's estate in every man."
or Yeats pacing the boards at Ballylee:
"How can we know the dancer from the dance?"

Thus, exegetes and preachers on their own
hold forth, against a never-ceasing din
of second-guessing, out there on their limbs:
Have faith! Behold, the mystery! Behold!

III
That fresco of the *Sermon on the Mount*
by Fra Angelico (dear brother John)
shows Jesus semicircled by his men,
gilt-haloed Galileans, but for one,

who will betray him later with a kiss,
atop their sandstone tuffets, rapt, engaged.
He's going on about beatitudes,
fulfillments of the law, the words to pray.
Outside the frame, unseen, a multitude
leans in to listen to the hermeneutics,
which are not without some challenges, to wit:
though we be smitten, turn the other cheek,
go the second mile, love our enemies;
while we're forgiven only so much as
we forgive those who trespass against us.
A certain eye-for-eyeness to that scheme,
a tooth-for-toothedness. A quid pro quo?
As if, to finally get, we must let go?
Sometimes it's so, sometimes it isn't? So,
what shall we say to these things? Who's to know?
Say who abides in love abides in God.
Say God is love. Love God. Love one another.
Say grace is undeserved and plentiful.
Say if we're saved, it's mostly from ourselves.[8]

Chapter Three

The Black Glacier

And this is the end,
the car running out of road,
the river losing its name in an ocean,
the long nose of the photographed horse
touching the white electronic line.
This is the colophon, the last elephant in the parade,
the empty wheelchair,
and pigeons floating down in the evening.
Here the stage is littered with bodies,
the narrator leads the characters to their cells,
and the climbers are in their graves.
It is me hitting the period
and you closing the book.
It is Sylvia Plath in the kitchen
and St. Clement with an anchor around his neck.
This is the final bit
thinning away to nothing.
This is the end, according to Aristotle,
what we have all been waiting for,
what everything comes down to,
the destination we cannot help imagining,
a streak of light in the sky,
a hat on a peg, and outside the cabin, falling leaves.[1]

So, we come, as all living beings do, to a contemplation of final details, end times, last things. "Is that all there is? Can it happen to me? Are we all alone? What comes next? Why is it cold?" These are the signatures of our species, the only ones that seem to know that the end is nearer than you think. The only ones who invent or keep faith in or hope for a life beyond the life they know is ending. Heaven, hell, Valhalla, Nirvana, the great mandala, the cloud of witnesses—we have dozens of constructs for the inkling of things that make us think we might haunt the future. Other days it seems there is nothing to it, a made-up thing, beyond belief. That we are all alone, that the dead are dead and gone. It's hard to know.

My own faith life is like a door that swings both ways on its hinges. Some days it seems like stating the obvious to say that we are children of a loving God who will bring us home to the hearth of our making and sit by the fire and listen as we tell the story of the lives we had. Others it seems like the dark is all around us, a darkness so replete, a silence beyond silence listened for.

I thought of walking round and round a space, writes the great Irish poet Seamus Heaney in the last of his "Clearances," a series of sonnets, eight of them, written in remembrance of his mother, who died in 1984.

> I thought of walking round and round a space
> Utterly empty, utterly a source
> Where the decked chestnut tree had lost its place
> In our front hedge above the wallflowers.
> The white chips jumped and jumped and skited high.
> I heard the hatchet's differentiated
> Accurate cut, the crack, the sigh
> And collapse of what luxuriated
> Through the shocked tips and wreckage of it all.
> Deep-planted and long gone, my coeval
> Chestnut from a jam jar in a hole,

Its heft and hush became a bright nowhere,
A soul ramifying and forever
Silent, beyond silence listened for.[2]

More than any writer of my generation and memory, I think that Heaney got good funerals right. He knew the difference between the honorific and the humane, between the heavy lift and thin gruel. He knew the difference between the idea of the thing and the thing itself.

Asked by his Boswell, Dennis O'Driscoll, why he traveled all the way to Krakow for the funeral of the Polish master, Czeslaw Milosz, Heaney said,

> Because he was a great poet who gave the art a noble profile. Because I loved and was strengthened by his work. Because I had come to know him better personally in the years before his death. Because I knew that, when I got to Krakow, I'd be among friends of his.[3]

Asked in the same interview about the difference between the memorial service, the ubiquitous "Celebration of Life" we now have grown accustomed to, and the funeral, Heaney is unambiguous:

> But memorial services are different from funerals. Funerals are closer to the bones, as it were; they have to deal with the rent in the fabric. The memorial service has more to do with the recompense of reputation, sometimes maybe with its retrieval. It's closer to the obituary notice than to the eternal questions.[4]

Heaney's poetry articulates these truths much better. Read "Funeral Rites," published at the height of the so-called Troubles—the sectarian war that raged in Heaney's North of Ireland between different sorts of Christians in the way that different sorts of Muslims have been at war throughout the Middle East for decades and centuries.

I shouldered a kind of manhood
stepping in to lift the coffins
of dead relations.
They had been laid out

in tainted rooms,
their eyelids glistening,
their dough-white hands
shackled in rosary beads.

Their puffed knuckles
had unwrinkled, the nails
were darkened, the wrists
obediently sloped.

The dulse-brown shroud,
the quilted satin cribs:
I knelt courteously
admiring it all

as wax melted down
and veined the candles,
the flames hovering
to the women hovering
behind me.
And always, in a corner,
the coffin lid,
its nail-heads dressed

with little gleaming crosses.
Dear soapstone masks,
kissing their igloo brows
had to suffice

before the nails were sunk
and the black glacier

of each funeral
pushed away.[5]

Our tribe did not read the Bible. We got it in doses, daily
or weekly, from a priest bound by the lectionary to give us
bits and pieces in collects, Epistles, Gospels, and graduals,
which, along with Confiteor and Kyrie, formed the front-
loaded, word-rich portion of the Tridentine Mass. These
were followed by sacred table work and common feed, to
wit laving and consecration, Communion, thanksgiving,
and benediction. On Sundays, it'd all be seasoned with some
lackluster homiletics (the Vatican, it is reported last week,
says eight minutes ought to be the limit), linked haphazardly
to the Scriptures on the day. These liturgies were labor-
intensive, heavy on metaphor and stagecraft, holy theater.
Possibly this is why few priests put much time into preaching, preferring, as the writing workshops say we ought, "to
show rather than to tell."

Still, we knew the stories: Eden and the apple, the murderous brother, the prodigal son, floods and leviathans,
mangers and magi, scribes and Pharisees and repentant
thieves. I remember my excitement the first time I heard
about the woman washing the Savior's feet with her tears,
wiping them with her long hair, and anointing them with
perfume. My father, a local undertaker, was especially fond
of Joseph of Arimathea and his sidekick, Nicodemus, who'd
bargained with Pilate for the corpse of Christ and tended to
the burial of same, in Joseph's own tomb, newly hewn from
rock, "in keeping with the customs of the Jews." My father
claimed this "a corporal work of mercy." This he'd been told
by the parish priest, who furthermore gave him what my
father called "a standing dispensation" from attendance at
Mass whenever he was called, as he fairly often was, to tend
to the dead and the bereaved on Sundays and Holy Days of
Obligation.

The biblical narratives were told and retold through our

formative years at school, by nuns who had done their little bit of editing and elaboration, the better to fit the pre-
dicaments of our station. And though we had a Bible at
home—an old counter-Reformation, Douay-Rheims translation from the Latin Vulgate of St. Jerome's fourth-century
text—we never read the thing. It was a holy knick-knack,
like the statue of the Blessed Mother, the picture of the
Sacred Heart, the table-top manger scene that came out for
Christmas, the crucifixes over each of our bedroom doors,
the holy water font at the front door—all designed to suit
our daily devotional lives. We prayed the family rosary in
May and October, kept the fasts and abstinences of Lent and
Advent along with whatever novena was in fashion and most
likely to inure to our spiritual betterments. We abstained
from meat on Friday, confessed our sins on Saturdays, kept
holy the Sabbath, such as we knew it, and basked in the
assurance that ours was the one true faith. Ours was a holy,
Roman, Irish-American, post-war-baby-booming, suburban family—sacramental, liturgical, replete with none-too-
subtle guilt and shaming, the big magic of transubstantiation, binding and loosing, the true presence, cardinal sins,
contrary virtues, states of grace, and the hope for salvation.
Litanies and chaplets stood in for Scriptures and hermeneutics. That was a thing the "other crowd" did, God-help-
them, bound to their idolatries about the Good Book, lost,
we reckoned, in the error of their ways.

I memorized, through the weekly instructions of Fr.
Thomas Kenny, the responses to the priests' incantations at
Mass, attracted as I was to the stately cadences of Latin and
the mystery of a secret language. I took up my service as an
altar boy at age seven, sharing duties for the 6:20 a.m. Mass
with my brothers, Dan and Pat, a year older and younger,
respectively, three weeks out of every four, at our parish
church, St. Columban's. Then we'd hustle off to Holy Name
School across town where the day's tutelage began with
a students' Mass at 8:15 read by the saintly, white-maned

Monsignor Paddock, beneath a huge mosaic on the general theme, the good sisters told us, of the Eucharist. Old Melchizedek was on one side and Abraham and Isaac on the other, prefiguring the risen Christ on his cross occupying the mosaic space between them—each a different version of priesthood, sacrifice, and Eucharist. This was the image I stared at all through the mornings of my boyhood, never knowing the chapters or verses I might have read for a more fulsome understanding of it all: how Abraham's willingness to sacrifice his son prefigured the death of Jesus on the cross; how the bloody business of worship and Communion became the loaf and cup of the Last Supper, and the priesthood of Melchizedek became the holy orders of churchmen down the centuries. Priesthood is something I understood in the cassocked and collared, biretta-topped celibates, the parish priests and curates, Jesuits and Franciscans in their habits who'd heard the voice of God—their vocation—and answered the call.

By twenty I was happily apostate, having come into my disbelief some few years after puberty, when a fellow pilgrim showed me all that she could on the exquisite mysteries of life. If the nuns had been wrong about sex, and they surely had been, it followed they were wrong on other things.

"Why do you reason about these things in your hearts?" Jesus asks the naysaying elders in Capernaum, in Mark's telling of the healing of a paralytic. They are trying to catch his blaspheming out, in the way we are always conniving against our spiritual betters.

I'd been named for a dead priest—my father's late Uncle Tom—and for the famously skeptical apostle, whose finger and dubiety still hover over the wounds of Christ, waiting, in the words of that great evangelist and voodoo economist, Ronald Reagan, to "trust but verify." True to which code, I questioned everything.

The deaths of innocents, the random little disasters that swept young mothers to their dooms in childbirth, their infants to their sudden crib deaths, young lovers to their demises in cars, perfect strangers to their hapless ends, seemed more evidence than anyone should need that whoever is in charge of these matters had a hit-and-miss record on humanity.

My work—I eventually got about my father's business— put me in earshot, albeit, over corpses, of some of the best preaching on theodicy available. The book of Job, however godawful and comfortless it is, remained for me a testament of faith: "blessed be the name of the Lord." Nonetheless, I remained devoutly lapsed in my confession and praxis.

So I was fairly shocked when years later, having achieved the rank of former husband and custodial father, small-town undertaker and internationally ignored poet, I got a call from one of my fellow Rotarians to say they were looking for "a good Catholic to join their Bible study."

"Let me know if you find one," is what I answered and we both laughed a little, but he persisted. "No, really, you'll like it. We're going to meet at the Big Boy Diner on Tuesday mornings at half past six. We'll be done by eight so everyone can get to work." Before I had time to construct a proper excuse he said, "See you then!" and hung up the phone.

What harm, I thought, it'll never last. A godawful hour and crummy eatery, not a great book, if a "good" one; like cocker spaniels, serviceable but ineluctably dull.

That was going thirty years ago. Our little study has outlived the restaurant, the Rotary, a few of our roughly dozen charter members, our denominations and divided politics, and still we meet—at my funeral home now—every early Tuesday morning, every season, every weather, to read and discuss various books of the Bible. We've done everything from Genesis to Revelation, all of the Gospels, some extra canonical texts, the letters of Paul. Job we've done three times, James maybe twice. We'll likely never do the Apocalypse again.

I only go to church now for baptisms, funerals, or weddings. The mysteries of birth and death and sex are regular
enough that I count as friends the neighborhood's clergy,
whose personal charities and heroics I've been eyewitness
to for many years. But dogma and dicta defy sound reason,
and the management class of the Church—all churches, for
that matter—seems uniquely wrong-headed and recklessly
feckless. What's more, my own views on same-sex marriage,
the ordination of women, priestly celibacy, and redemptive
suffering, would put me so sufficiently at odds with them as
to render me, no doubt, an ex-communicant.

Oddly enough, the less observant I became, in belief or
devotion, the better the "good" book seemed to me. I didn't
need the religious epic so much as a good story, something
to share, a party piece.

I can't remember not knowing about the healing of the
paralytic, whether I heard it at Mass or from one of the nuns
or Christian brothers who were in charge of my education,
or read it as part of our Bible study. There it is, in three
Gospels out of four, the details more or less the same. It is
one of the three dozen or so miracle stories that punctuate the New Testament, from changing water into wine at
Cana, calming the storm and filling the fishnets, to healings
of lepers and the blind and lame and raising the dead, himself included. There are endless demons and devils cast out,
sins forgiven, apparitions after his death. It was a poem in
a book published a few years back that brought it newly to
life for me.

The last time I heard Seamus Heaney read was in the
Glenn Memorial Chapel at Emory University. It was and
remains a Methodist church, which doubles as an auditorium for gatherings of a certain size. It was the 2nd of March
of 2013 and I was occupying the McDonald Family Chair at
Candler School of Theology at Emory University, teaching
a course with the great preacher and theologian, Thomas
Long, on "The Poetics of the Sermon." Dr. Long and I were

just putting the final touches on a book we'd coauthored called *The Good Funeral*, due out later that year. And I was learning words like exegesis and hermeneutics and studying the dynamics of fiction, which Dr. Long regarded as a workable template for homiletics. We examined narrative arc and point of view, plot and character and setting. We read poems and short fictions and published sermons.

I was delighted that Heaney would be coming to town. His had been the most amplified and ever-present voice of my generation of poets. His work, since I first encountered it forty-five years ago, reading by the fire in the ancestral home in County Clare I would later inherit, had never failed to return a rich trove and metaphoric treasures. Because so much of his poetry came out of a Catholic upbringing in rural Ireland, he became for me a useful guide for the parish of language and imagination.

Possibly because I first encountered prayer as poetry, or at least as language cast in rhyme and meter, addressed to the heavens as a sort of raised speech, poetry had always seemed sacerdotal, proper for addressing the mysteries of happenstance and creation. M. Craig Barnes had framed this notion of the ministerial life in his book *The Pastor as Minor Poet*, seeming to draw close to the notion that poets and pastors were undertakers too.

That Heaney held the natural world and human work—the chore and toil of the mundane, earthbound and near-to-hand—in awe and reverence seemed more attuned to the holy than the politicized religiosity of the culture. Still, the Latin I'd learned as an altar boy in the 1950s—the sacraments, devotions, and sensibilities I'd been raised with—found many echoes in the early poems of the Irish master, even if my own life's experience and further examinations of Scripture and secular texts had left me if not entirely apostate, then less a believer and more a beholder. Though freighted with doubts and wonders and religiously adrift, I treasured the language of faith as an outright gift—the

hymns of Charles Wesley, the angel-wrestling contemplations of John Calvin, the thundering Scots rectitude of John
Knox, the exile and anchoritic adventures of Columcille, and
the rubrics of holy women and men—I retained some level
of religious literacy given me by nuns and Christian brothers, but rejected the magisterium of the church. By the time
I'd arrived at Emory in the late winter of 2013 I was deeply
devoted to a church of latter-day poets, skeptics, and non-
compliant but kindly sorts. The irony of such a backslidden
fellow as myself teaching at a school of theology, named for
the Methodist bishop and first chancellor of Emory whose
brother was the owner of our national sugar water, Coca-
Cola, was not lost on me. Though I had been schooled in my
apostasy by H. L. Mencken, Robert Ingersoll, Christopher
Hitchens, and Richard Dawkins, and by the feckless malfeasance of bishops and abusive priests, I had also witnessed,
over four decades in funeral service, the everyday heroics
of the reverend clergy and their coreligionists. These were
men and women of faith who showed up whenever there was
trouble. Their best preaching was done when the chips were
down, in extremis, at death beds, in the hospitals and nursing homes and family homes and funeral homes. They pitch
in and do their part even though they cannot fix the terrible
things that happen. They are present, they pray, they keep
open the possibility of hope. And I'd been schooled by my
semester among the Methodists and seminarians at Emory,
and by my friendship with the Rev. Thomas Long, whose
scholarship and work in words has re-formed me in a way I
thought impossible.

Thus, Heaney's reading from the raised sanctuary of
Glenn Memorial Chapel seemed a "keeping holy" of a Sabbath, and his poems, portions of a sacred text. And when he
said, deep into what would be one of his last public readings,
that he'd like to read some poems from his "last book," and
then corrected himself to say, "my most recent collection,"
I thought the insertion of the shadow of death was a deft

touch by a seasoned performer of his work. It is also true that his "most recent collection," *Human Chain*, seemed so haunted a book, dogged by death and impendency and the urgency of last things.

On that day he read one of my favorites of his poems. "Miracle" proposes a shift of focus in the scriptural story of Jesus healing the paralytic, my favorite rendition of which occurs in Mark 2:1–12. Jesus is preaching in Capernaum and the crowd is so great, filling the room and spilling out the door into the street, that four men bringing the paralytic to be healed have to hoist him up to the roof, remove the roof tiles or dig through the sod, and lower him down on his bed by ropes, whereupon Jesus, impressed by their faith, tells the poor cripple his sins are forgiven. Of course, the begrudgers among them—and there are always begrudgers—begin to mumble among themselves about blasphemy, because, "Who can forgive sins but God alone?" Jesus questions them, saying, "Which is easier?"—by which he means, the lesser miracle—"to say, 'your sins are forgiven you,' or to say, 'Arise, take up your bed and walk'?" (NKJV) It is, of course, a trick question.

Because forgiveness seems impossible, whether to give or to receive, and impossible to see. It would always take a miracle. Nor is God the only one capable of forgiving. Do we not pray to be forgiven our trespasses "as we forgive those who trespass against us"? Who among us is not withered and weighed down by the accrual of actual or imagined slights, betrayals, resentments, estrangements, and wrongdoings done unto us most often by someone we've loved? And in ways I needn't number, we're all paralyzed, hobbled by our grievances and heartbreaks, by the press of sin, the failure of vision, by fear, by worry, by anxieties about the end.

Whereas the Scripture directs our attention to the paralytic, and to the quibbles between Jesus and the scribes, Heaney's poem bids us be mindful of the less learned toil and utterly miraculous decency of "the ones who have

known (us) all along," who lift us up, bear us in our broken-
ness, and get us where we need to go. On any given day it
seems miracle enough.

The everyday and deeply human miracle, void of heavenly hosts or interventions, has especial meaning for Heaney
who, in August of 2006, woke up in a guest house in Donegal paralyzed by a stroke. The day before he had attended
the birthday party for Anne Friel, wife of the playwright
and Heaney's schoolmate and lifelong friend, Brian Friel.
After the night's festivities, the Heaneys spent the night with
other friends and fellow poets in the local bed and breakfast.
He awakened to paralysis on the left side of his body. So it
was his wife, Marie, and Des and Mary Kavanagh, Peter and
Jean Fallon and Tom Kilroy—ones who had known him all
along—who helped strap him on to the gurney and get him
down the steep stairs, out of the building and into the waiting
ambulance to ride with his wife to Letterkenny Hospital. In
the poem, which took shape in the weeks of what he called
"rest cure" in the Royal Hospital, Donnybrook, in Dublin,
the narrative power proceeds: "Not the one who takes up
his bed and walks," but rather, to "the ones who have known
him all along and carry him in," who do the heavy lifting of
his care and transport. They are the agents of rescue and
restoration, their faithful friendship miraculous and salvific.
Their hefting and lifting and large muscle work is the stuff
and substance of salvation. Here is the short poem.

MIRACLE

Not the one who takes up his bed and walks
But the ones who have known him all along
And carry him in—

Their shoulders numb, the ache and stoop deeplocked
In their backs, the stretcher handles
Slippery with sweat. And no let-up

> Until he's strapped on tight, made tiltable
> and raised to the tiled roof, then lowered for healing.
> Be mindful of them as they stand and wait
>
> For the burn of the paid-out ropes to cool,
> Their slight lightheadedness and incredulity
> To pass, those ones who had known him all along.[6]

This language of shoulders, aching backs, and waiting for the burn of paid-out ropes to cool honors the hands-on, whole-body habits of human labor the poet learned as a farm boy in Derry. From comparing his father's spade work in the turf bog to his own excavations in meaning and language in his poem "Digging," to the town and country indentures of blacksmithing, well-gazing, and kite-flying at the end of "Human Chain," Heaney's work upholds the holiness of human labor and the sacred nature of the near-to-hand.

Hearing its maker read "Miracle" from the pulpit at Emory put me in mind of my conversation with him at the funeral of our friend, Dennis O'Driscoll, who had died less than three months before, on Christmas Eve, 2012, and was buried near his home in Naas, County Kildare.

Seamus had been Dennis's principal eulogist on the day, just as Dennis had been Heaney's most insightful interlocutor. His book of interviews with Heaney, *Stepping Stones*, is the nearest thing to an autobiography we will ever have of the Nobel Laureate, and more thoroughly than ever examines the life of the man in relation to the work.

Following O'Driscoll's funeral liturgy, I walked with Heaney and his wife in the sad cortege from the church to the cemetery, half a mile or so, following the coffin and the other mourners. We chatted about our dead friend and the sadness we all shared. Maybe Heaney's stroke six years before and my open-heart surgery the year before eventuated in our bringing up the rear of the entourage. We were taking our time, huffing and puffing some at the steeper bits, as we made our slow but steady way up the town, out the road, to the grave behind the hearse. In Ireland the dead are shouldered to the opened ground and lowered in with ropes by the pallbearers. After the priest has had his say, the grave is filled in by family and friends. The miracle of life and the mystery of death are unambiguously tethered by a funiculus of grave ropes and public grieving, religiously bound by the exercise of large muscle duties—shoulder and shovel work and the heart's indentures, each a linkage in the ongoing, unbroken human chain. And the strain of pallbearers at O'Driscoll's open grave, as they lowered his coffined body into the opened ground, slowly paying out the ropes, seemed like the faithful and existential labor of the paralytic's friends, lowering his bed through the opened roof in Capernaum to the foot of his healer for a cure.

The witness of these things drew a catch in my breath that New Year's Eve morning when we buried Dennis O'Driscoll, in the new row of St. Corban's Cemetery. Watching his pallbearers lower him into the vacancy of the grave, these mundane mortuary chores replicating the miraculous narrative of the Gospels where the paralytic's pals lower him into the place of his healing, the "slight lightheadedness and incredulity" perfectly articulated in Heaney's poem, remains caught in my chest, not yet exhaled. And like the scribes in Capernaum, that day in Naas, though I'd seen such things all my workaday life, I'd "never seen anything like this before."

And yet I saw it all again, months later in the late summer when Heaney's death stunned us all on Friday morning, the 30th of August, 2013. I woke to texts and emails from Dublin. "Seamus is dead," is what they read. "Ah, hell . . ." I wrote back. Ah, hell, indeed.

I called David Fanagan, the Dublin undertaker, and asked if I might ride in the hearse. Someone who knew the poems and the poet should ride along.

I flew to Shannon and stayed at my digs in Clare that night and drove up to Dublin on Sunday morning, stopping in Naas to visit Dennis's grave. At Fanagan's in Aungier Street, Heaney was laid out in Chapel 3, the corpse, horizontal and still, "silent beyond silence listened for." Marie greeted me and thanked me for making the long journey and was a little shocked to hear that I'd had my ticket in hand for more than a month, long before Seamus had any notion of dying. She told me she thought he must have had a heart attack on Wednesday, complaining of a pain in his jaw, then tripped leaving a restaurant on Thursday, which got him to the hospital where they discovered a tear in his aorta. The only thing more risky than operating, she was told, was doing nothing. He was in extremis. A team was assembled to do the procedure at half past seven on Friday morning, just minutes before which he texted her, calm and grateful for the long years of love, and told her not to be afraid. "Noli timere" he wrote at the end, the ancient language, in English: Be not afraid. He was dead before the operation began.

All the way up there people lined the way, on the overpasses, and in the halted intersections where people got out of their cars to applaud the cortege of the great poet. Women were weeping or wiping tears from their faces. Men held the palms of their hands to their hearts, caps doffed, thumbs up, everyone at their best attention.

"How did you get to be the one?" I asked the man at the wheel of the new Mercedes-Benz hearse, no doubt hustled into service for the TV cameras. "I drew the short straw," he told me. "We used to get extra to drive in the North, what with the Troubles and fanatics. Now it's just a long haul and a long day."

We picked up forty or fifty cars as we made our way, the roughly three-hour drive north from Dublin, then west around Belfast making for Derry, crossing the river that connects Lough Beg to Lough Neagh at Toomebridge, the crowds getting bigger the nearer we got. Police on motorcycles picked us up at the border, just outside of Newry, and

escorted our makeshift motorcade all the way to the cemetery as we went down the boreen off the main road and
drove by the family farm and onward to Bellaghy, where a
piper met us at the entrance to town and piped us through
the village. The crowd spilled out of shops and pubs and
houses and into the road, every man, woman, and child out
applauding, crossing themselves, giving out with bits of
"Danny Boy" and holding their hearts in signals of respect.
The sadness on their faces and the tribute to the level man
behind me in the box was like nothing I'd ever seen, and
when we got to the grave, led there by a cadre of churchmen
in white albs and copes and cowls, I took the family spray
up to the grave through the cordons of paparazzi clicking
photos of everything. I walked with Marie and her family
behind the coffin as we went to the grave, where against
my hopes that Seamus would pop out and proclaim it all a
big mistake, his sons and his brothers and her brothers bent
to the black ropes and lowered him into the ground, the
paid-out ropes and the burn in their arms and hands and
the hush of the gathered multitude notwithstanding. Leaves
rustled in the overarching sycamores. The clergy struck up a
verse of "Salve Regina" to re-insinuate their imprimatur on
it all. We hung around in that sad and self-congratulatory
way mourners do, after the heavy lifting is done. The limo
had a slow leak in the right front tire that had to be tended
to. Des Kavanagh and his wife, Mary, came and spoke to me,
wondering if I'd be in Galway anytime soon. Brian Friel's
car pulled away; he nodded. Michael, Seamus's son, came
over to thank me for going in the hearse with his dad, and I
was glad of that. And grateful. I stayed until the sod was back
on him, and the flowers sorted on top of that, and then we
drove back the road, arriving in Dublin right around dark.
Anthony MacDonald, his short-straw, long day nearing its
end, dropped me at the corner of Georges Street and Ste-
phen Street Lower. I gave him some cash and told him to
get something at the off license with my thanks for taking

me up and back on the day, for getting Seamus where he needed to go, and getting me where I needed to be. "No bother," he said, "Not a bit." Nothing out of the utterly ordinary, utterly pedestrian, a miracle.

Possibly these are the miracles we fail to see, on the lookout as we are for signs and wonders: for seas that part for us to pass through, skies that open to a glimpse of heaven, the paralytic who stands and walks, the blind who begin to see, the shortfall that becomes a sudden abundance. Maybe what we miss are the ordinary miracles, the ones who have known us all along—the family and friends, the fellow pilgrims who show up, pitch in and do their parts to get us where we need to go, within earshot and arms' reach of our healing, the earthbound, everyday miracle of forbearance and forgiveness, the help in dark times to light the way, the ones who turn up when there is trouble to save us from our hobbled, heart-wrecked selves.

Some years ago, I took it in my mind to write a sonnet on every birthday, the better to measure the passing of time by keeping track of those sonnets. The resolve, like most resolves, lasted one year, and actually when I inspected the text of that year's assignment I noticed I'd come to fifteen lines, which amplifies the point I suppose that the older we get the less we count. The miscalculation supplied, however, a title for an errant poem, to wit, "Refusing at Fifty-two to Write Sonnets." So,

REFUSING AT FIFTY-TWO TO WRITE SONNETS

It came to him that he could nearly count
How many Octobers he had left to him
In increments of ten or, say, eleven
Thus, sixty-three, seventy-four, eighty-five.
He couldn't see himself at ninety-six—

Humanity's advances notwithstanding
In health care, self help or New Age regimens—
What with his habits and family history,
The end he thought is nearer than you think.

The future, thus confined to its contingencies,
The present moment opens like a gift:
The balding month, the grey week, the blue morning,
The hour's routine, the minute's passing glance—
All seem like godsends now. And what to make of this?
At the end the word that comes to us is Thanks.[7]

Thanks.

Chapter Four

Some Thoughts on Uteri, on Wombs

The contemplation of the womb, like staring into the starlit heavens, fills me with imaginings of Something-ness or Nothingness. It was ever thus. If space is the final frontier, the womb is the first one—that place where, to borrow Wallace Stevens's phrase, the idea of the thing becomes the thing itself. It is the tabernacle of our expectations. The seedbed and safe harbor whence we launch, first home and habitat, the garden of delight's denouement. A place where the temps are set, the rent is easy, the food is good, and we aren't bothered by telephone or tax man. That space we are born out of, into the world, where the soft iambics of our mother's heart become the first sure verses of our being, the first poetry of our life, Cavafy said. "Sometimes they speak to us in dreams. Sometimes deep in thought the mind hears them. . . . like music at night, distant, fading away."

When I first beheld, as a student in mortuary school, plates 60 and 61 in book five of *De humani corporis fabrica libri septem* —The Fabric of the Human Body—by the great sixteenth-century physician and anatomist, Andreas Vesalius, I was smitten with ontological and existential awe. A disciple of the first-century Greek philosopher and medico, Galen of Pergamon, one sees in the Belgian's handiwork the male gaze on female parts he examines at autopsy and vivisection. There is such tenderness in the splayed cavity and skinned breast of the headless woman of his scrutiny, such precision to his illustrations of her innards.

By then I'd had a rudimentary acquaintance with the bodies of women. I knew what to touch and rub, fondle and savor, hug and hold, loosen and let go, lave and graze. But the frank exposure of the human fabric that Vesalius's images detailed were wondrous to me, unveiling as they do, apocalyptically, the beauty of both form and function. Had I not found his drawings so sumptuously instructive—corresponding as they did to the focus of my own gobsmacked gaze—I might have considered then what I consider now, here in my age and anecdotage, to wit, the notion that, though each gender has its own specific parts to play in our species' drama of "reproduction," such issues are neither male nor female solely. Rather, they are human in scope and nature, requiring, in both meaning and performance, the two it always takes to tango. We are, it turns out, in this together.

Still, it is impossible to behold a woman's parts without gratitude and awe. Likewise I am often chuffed—a word which means both one thing and its opposite—by the sense such encounters invariably include that we are all, in fact, the same but different, the anatomists' renderings of our private parts shows the male member is nothing so much as a vagina turned inside out, so that the adventitia, smooth muscle and mucosa of the latter reflect, actually, the phallic urgency of the former, almost as if they were made for each other, bespoke, custom fit —like sword to scabbard, hand to glove, preacher to pulpit or corpse to opened ground.

And, lest any man assume the sword more salient than the scabbard, consider science, that great leveler.

In utero, we all start as female and only the random happenstance of the Y chromosome and its attendant hormones makes some of us male. Still, testes are unambiguously fallen ovaries and the scrotal raphe a labial scar from the fusion of one's formerly female lips. The penis is a clitoris writ large, the nipples sans lactating, ornaments for men to remind them of the truth they are mostly boobs that do not work. So, whether penetration, ejaculation, ovulation, uterine contraction, fertilization, or gestation seals the reproductive deal, each is essential to this essential mystery, we are brought into being by the fervent collaboration of both male and female. Science provides stand-ins for the stallion and sire. "They bring the bull in a suitcase, now," my cousin Nora in West Clare informed me years ago, speaking of her small troupe of milking Friesians, which had a withering effect upon my rampant mannishness. Men are easily made redundant but female mammals still do the heavy bearing. Far from the second, weaker sex, the female seems the first and fiercest, like poetry to language, the one without which nothing happens.

I went for stillborn babies, as a boy. Well not a boy, exactly, but not yet a man. My apprenticeship to my father's business meant I'd go to hospitals to get the tiny lifeless bodies, transported in a small black box, such as one might take fishing or keep one's tools. I'd return them to the funeral home: wee incubates in various stages of incompleteness and becoming. Sometimes they were so perfectly formed in miniature that they seemed like tiny icons of humanity, their toes and fingers, noses and eyes, their little selves too small, too still, but otherwise perfectly shaped and made. As with Galen and Vesalius, as with Wallace Stevens, the thing itself outweighs the idea of the thing. Thus, these little fetal things, stillborn or born but not quite viable, were freighted with a gravitas, fraught with sadness, laden with a desolation born of dashed hopes and grave-bound humanity. The body, the incarnate thing, is critical to our understanding. The uterus is wellspring, headwater, home ground of our being.

In time, I'd learn to sit with the families of dead fetuses, dead toddlers, dead teenagers—the parents who'd outlived the ones they'd made, the fathers who remembered the night of bliss they'd had, the kissing and embraces, the mothers who recalled their first intuitions of gravity, their gravidness, its gravitas, the grave consequences of impregnation—an ill-at-easeness in their lower core, tenderness in the breast, the momentary hot flash of a future changed or changing utterly.

"It's only been maybe a hundred years," says my young assistant, halfway through her childbearing years, "that women have actually owned their uteri." And even now, she adds, the agency of men—of husbands and fathers, bishops and politicos, no less moguls and marketeers—have too much a say in what goes on in the hidden places of a woman's body, the womb and its attendant, adjacent parts: cervix, ovaries, fallopian tubes, the adventitia, clitoris, labia major and minor, the mons pubis, all of which conspire, as it were, to raise a chorus of praise to the mighty nature whereby we renew, repeat, reproduce, and replicate ourselves.

In the panel *Eve Tempted by the Serpent* by Defendente Ferrari, who was painting in Turin whilst Vesalius was dissecting in Padua, the pale-skinned, naked teenager's mons veneris is obscured by the filigree leaf frond of the sapling she is plucking an apple from—the tree of knowledge of good and evil. The leering, bearded, lecherous, old-mannish faced snake, slithering up the adjacent tree, is hissing his temptation in her ear. It is the last moment of paradise, the girl in her girlish innocence, oblivious to the ramifications; her genitalia, her tiny breasts, her consort's parts are not yet shameful. Time will eventually blame everything on her: the fall of humanity, the pain of childbirth, the provocations of her irrepressible beauty, death itself. But for now, God is still happy with creation. He has looked about and seen that it was good. It's all written down in Genesis 3. The diptych panel with Adam, perhaps erect and prelapsarian, has been lost to the centuries, so we do not see how happy he is, how willing and ready and grateful he is for her succor and company, her constancy.

It was the drizzling morning in the winter of 1882, in Washington, DC, a retinue of black-clad pilgrims gathered around a small grave in the Congressional Cemetery to bury little Harry Miller, a toddling boy who had succumbed to that season's contagion of diphtheria. The small coffin rested on the ropes and boards over the open ground while the mother's sobs worked their way into a rising crescendo. The undertaker nodded to the man at the head of the grave to begin. He shook his head. The mother's animal sobs continued. She was bent over, like someone stabbed, wrapping her small arms round her uncorseted middle, holding herself together by dint of will at the point in her body where she felt the blade of her bereavement most keenly.

"Does Mrs. Miller desire it?" the speaker asked. The dead boy's father nodded his assent.

The officiant on the day was Robert Ingersoll, the most notorious disbeliever of his time, his age's Christopher Hitchens, Richard Dawkins, or Bill Maher. Though stridently unchurched, Ingersoll was the son of the manse, the youngest son of a Congregationalist minister who preached his abolitionist views, and had, as a consequence, been given his walking papers by congregants around the East and Midwest. Robert spent most of his youth shifting from church to church because of his father's politics. Because of his father's mistreatment at the hands of Congregationalists, Robert turned first on Calvinism and then on Christianity and, by the time he stepped to the head of the grave that rainy morning in Washington, DC, he was the best-known infidel in America—an orator and lecturer who had traveled the country upholding humanism, "free thinking and honest talk" and making goats of religionists and their ecclesiastical up-lines.

"Preaching to bishops," a priest of my acquaintance once told me, "is like farting at skunks." And I wonder now if he wasn't quoting Robert Green Ingersoll. As he stepped to the head of the Miller boy's burial site, Ingersoll began his oration.

I know how vain it is to gild a grief with words, and yet I
wish to take from every grave its fear. . . . From the wondrous tree of life the buds and blossoms fall with ripened
fruit, and in the common bed of earth patriarchs and babes
sleep side by side. . . .
Every cradle asks us "Whence?" and every coffin
"Whither?" . . .
They who stand with breaking hearts around this little
grave, need have no fear. . . .
We have no fear; we are all children of the same mother
and the same fate awaits us all. We, too, have our religion,
and it is this: Help for the living, hope for the dead.[1]

Help for the living. Hope for the dead.

Every cradle asks us whence indeed, and every coffin
whither. The abyss we consign our dead to—opened ground
or fire, pond or sea or air—is incubation of a sort our sacred
texts make faith claims for, hoping they are like the space,
pear shaped sometimes, no more than centimeters, hor-
monally engaged, impregnated by mighty nature—a primal
station in the journey of our being.

What bent the dead boy's mother over was the grief, felt
most keenly in her most hidden places, the good earthen,
opened seedbed of her uterus, vacated with pushing and
with pain, and vanquished utterly by her child's death. It
is the desolation Eve must have felt, when one of her sons
killed the other. And the wonder Andreas Vesalius beheld
when looking into the bloody entrails of the Paduan girl
who first unveiled for him the mystery of our coming into
being; and by the sound and sense we humans get, examin-
ing our lexicon, that "grave" and "gravid" share their page
and etymology, no less gravitas and gravity; "grace" and
"gratitude." And that the surest human rhymes of all are
"womb" and "tomb."

Chapter Five

Euclid and the Properties of Love and Eucharist

(On Michael Heffernan)

M ost mornings in Milford for the past thirty years I've gone to coffee with the same bunch of men—a couple dozen local moguls and professional sorts—attorneys and bankers, chiropractors and politicos, estate agents and retailers, old soldiers and sailors and marines, assembled around a long table with our oatmeal and rye toast, poached eggs and blather. Some do the boiled breakfast, some the fry.

Nowadays, all but a couple of us are retired. I'm still full time. Some days I do corpses and hearses; others it's sentences and pentameters. "Old farts" I call us, for the way our talk has gone from the emergent and needful to the chronic and mundane. Important discourses on staff management, business and mission statements have given way to colloquies on golf and sleep apnea, the price of petrol and flatulence, the pharmaceuticals of urination, blood sugar, and stool softeners.

As I am the youngest among them, I see in them harbingers of my own devolution: the predictable routines of aging and decrepitude, memory and the loss of it. Men of a certain age, I've come to believe, for all their vainglories and redundancies, have plenty to tell us, much the same as women: some days they bore and others they inspire.

What sort of morning was Euclid having
when he first considered parallel lines?
Or that business about how things equal
to the same thing are equal to each other?
Who's to know what the day has in it?
This morning Bert took it into his mind
to make a long bow out of Osage orange
and went on eBay to find the cow horns
from which to fashion the tips of the thing.
You better have something to pass the time,
he says, stirring his coffee, smiling.[1]

Whether I wrote these lines, from a poem I called
"Euclid," before or after my friend and mentor, the poet
Michael Heffernan, sent me his poem, called "Geometric,"
is hard to know. Here are a few of his opening lines:

Euclid became my savior in tenth grade,
the year the Jesuits wanted me a priest.
They sent me to Manresa in Birmingham
and put me in a room with a radiator
that knocked all night to keep me up for prayer,
nothing for breakfast, not a thing for lunch
and barley soup and Wonder bread for supper.

It was no wonder then that Euclid cried
out of this darkness of mortification
in a squared circle with a human face
that set me right about four equal lines
drawn from a radius the square root of pi
this being God as Dante painted Him,
and good enough for me to believe in
in place of hellfire and my going there,
because, as I recall, that square was purple,
a color I can see, though color blind,

as I have been since the wet grass was red
after a rain when I was four years old.
That was the spring of 1947.[2]

It was the fall of 1967. Heff was going on twenty-five and
I was not quite nineteen—his first teaching job and my second lackluster college year put us both in the same place at
the same time. We've been friends and correspondents ever
since.

Our Euclidian poems—Heffernan's and mine—are but
current renditions of the chicken and egg sort of collabora-
tive fare our near half a century of correspondence has produced. For reasons I may never understand, poetry has been
our responsorial task, like archpriest and acolyte—each of us
trying for the first word or the last. Like the Latin we both
heard at daily Mass, or the running tally accountants keep:
some lines in the red ink, some in black.

Writers, I've said more than once, are readers who
karaoke. They find a tune that moves them and they try
to sing along. Eventually they begin to sound like themselves talking to themselves. They are said, at this point, to
have found their voice, when in fact what they've found are
maybe a hundred voices or a dozen, that seem, every one of
them, one of a kind.

All writing begins with this indebtedness—to someone
who made you wish you'd written that thing yourself: the
last paragraph of Joyce's "The Dead" or that thing Emily
Dickinson wrote about "first chill, then stupor, then the let-
ting go," or Montaigne when he conjectured: "In every man
is the whole of man's estate." Or maybe it is something from
the book of Job. We all have our lists of overdrawn accounts,
those we could never repay beyond the words we keep adding to the general register of words that are, like things in a
library, to be borrowed and returned.

To be among the elegant voices of those who made us

think that language could be transformative, transubstantial, medicinal, and magic—those ones we hear humming from the books in our possession—that is why we write, because we read. We learn to speak by keeping our ears tuned to the language of our species.

Heffernan was the first on my list and introduced me to Yeats and Emerson and Melville and Whitman, and dozens of others to whom I owe the way my ear was eventually tuned to the language.

> And Murray is carving a model truck
> from a block of walnut he found downstairs.
> Whittling away he thinks of the years
> he drove between Detroit and Buffalo
> delivering parts for General Motors.
> Might he have nursed theorems on lines and dots
> or the properties of triangles or
> the congruence of adjacent angles?
> Or clearing customs at Niagara Falls,
> arrived at some insight on wholes and parts
> or an axiom involving radii
> and the making of circles, how distance
> from a center point can be both increased
> endlessly and endlessly split—a mystery
> whereby the local and the global share
> the same vexations and geometry?[3]

All poets borrow, said Eliot years ago; great poets steal! Thus "Nuns Fret Not at Their Convent's Narrow Room," which was Wordsworth's sonnet of praise for sonnets, begets a sonnet in a book of mine called "Corpses Do Not Fret Their Coffin Boards."

And when we are not stealing, maybe it's translating so Heaney brings Beowulf out of old English and the birdman, Sweeney, back to life and Robin Robertson "Englishes" the great Swede, Tomas Tranströmer, and Akhmatova translates Rabindranath Tagore, Khaled Mattawa, a Libyan friend, brings the Syrian master, Adonis, to Michigan and America.

"Like dropping a rose petal down the Grand Canyon," said Don Marquis about publishing poems, "and waiting for the echo." And isn't it so? An act of faith or madness: to think it might matter, might make a difference, that trope or notion that woke you in the middle of a dark time to write it down—lines or bits of lines that made so much sense in the dream, but in the daylight seem to need a cipher.

Surely it was Bishop Berkeley's tree, the one that fell so noiselessly in the forest, its very being requiring a godly witness because no one on the planet really cares—surely the paper on which poetry is made is wrought from trees that no one ever heard of. "Poetry"—again Marquis—"is what Milton saw when he went blind."

Who, you are possibly asking yourself, is Don Marquis? A man who wrote poems, a tree that fell in the forest. And Milton? Who's to know?

And yet we have our echo chambers—the sounds and sense we keep making to the curious few who keep language alive through poetry. Poets read poets. And it is rare to find a review of poetry that isn't done by a practitioner.

It was Michael Heffernan who made me want to write poems. It was seeing his poems go from handwritten notes to typed clean copy to publication in literary journals to the book that made its way down the road in the postman's bag more than thirty years ago. I remember holding it in my hand: *The Cry of Oliver Hardy*, it was called—sixty-one pages on fine paper and serviceable binding by a respectable university press. I remember holding it and knowing that the poems, thus enclosed, would find their way into bookshops and libraries and private collections, and whatever sounds they made, this configuration of his voice would outlive him. And I remember thinking, I'd like some record of my own, to leave to my sons and daughter.

He thought about the things he knew for sure
how men were lonely and lived lonely lives
how even the sun was lonely and on fire
He thought about the cry of Oliver Hardy
how he would dance with dread and tweedle his derby
and send his clear soprano up from all his tonnage
whenever the deadly husband with the knives
the murderous sailor or their own relentless wives
were about to do him and his pal some permanent
damage.[4]

These lines from a sonnet in a series of sonnets Heff
called "The Crazyman's Revival" in that first book of his got
me thinking and speaking in iambs and trochees, in utter-
ances of ten or eleven or a dozen syllables, which seemed a
breath's worth of my best articulations.

And at mornings over coffee with the old farts I often see
us all as versions of Stan and Ollie, laughable in the near
term, tragic at a distance, as Charlie Chaplin always said
we'd be.

The collaboration between Michael Heffernan and me
was essential to my work in words. When I first sent poems
off to be published, it was to journals recommended by him.
When I first had enough published work to proffer a book-
length manuscript, it was mailed off to editors and presses
at addresses Heffernan gave to me and just as many of the
poems in his books have been written in response to mine,
no few of mine have been responses to his. Thus, the book
of mine titled *Walking Papers*, with poems like "Red," and
"Asleep," and "On a Bar of Chinese Soap," prefigure poems
in the book Michael Heffernan recently wrote with poems
like "Purple," and "Awake" and "A Bar of Chinese Soap";
indeed, the first poem in my first book addresses the "crazy
man," revived in Heffernan's first book. In "Michael's Reply
to the White Man," my head case proclaims:

Listen mister, I'm not one of those
who feels prenatal in the tub or has
some trauma in his childhood to account
for what it is that dogs me now. I do
no drugs nor booze except the sociables,
to blow the wondrous coals in me to flame
to where I sing songs, talk in tongues, fix names
to hitherto unknown things. Syllables
are the things I do and do them carefully
so the great-grandkids of folks like you
will have something from this dire century
besides Freud and wars and hula hoops.
See what I'm really after is that tune
God hummed that Monday when he made the world.[5]

The search for that breath of God, that inspiration,
involves as much as anything the faith that language is itself
imbued with the fiery, Pentecostal tongue of creation we
frame in the familiar biblical trope: in the beginning was the
word and the word became flesh.

That was the spring of 1947.
[Heff's "Geometrics" carries on:]
My grandmother had lathered the lye soap
the way she would when I said damn or shit,
and I ran up the stairs to the closet
I always hid in when she got the suds
And never could find out where I was hiding.
That circled square is purple in my mind
because I can't see Euclid colorless.
This purple borders him upon his throne
of lordly order the geometer
alone encompasses in his mind's eye.
I can't remember whether Euclid ever
attempted squaring the circle, though he must have.

It wasn't something Father Loetze covered.
He was the one before Theology
who told us Euclid looked on Beauty naked,
meaning to shock us, while he tapped the board
in perfect classic Solid Geometry,
his chalky soutane flying with his back turned,
and nothing for it but a reverie
about the breasts of Emil Bogen's daughter
and whether they were perfect cones or spheres.
Her father was a tailor up the street.
He often stood in front on the sidewalk
rolling a piece of chalk between his palms.
He made it crack against his wedding ring.
Behind him the mannequins have nothing on
but open-toed high heels and strings of pearls.[6]

And though Heff's "Euclid" meditates on youth whereas
mine seems fixed more so on age, both come round to
dwelling on the words made flesh, in either case, the breasts
of women:

Possibly this is where God comes into it,
who breathed the common notion of coincidence
into the brain of that Alexandrian
over breakfast twenty-three centuries back,
who glimpsed for a moment that morning the sense
it all made: life, killing time, the elements,
the dots and lines and angles of connection—
an egg's shell opened with a spoon, the sun's
connivance with the moon's decline, Sophia
the maidservant pouring juice; everything,
everything coincides, the arc of memory,
her fine parabolas, the bend of a bow,
the curve of the earth, the turn in the road.[7]

And now it is the autumn of 2017. Heffernan and I have been pals for fifty years and the count of our books on shelves in libraries is well into the double figures—poems, stories, essays, plays—the stanzas, sentences, the characters and words we've put into characters' mouths.

We write because we cannot keep from writing. And when we don't write, we read. Language is our shared idolatry, like that index finger in the Michelangelo, pointing and pronouncing the names of things, as if we could decode all mystery if we are patient enough for the words to come, in the way that Euclid might've waited on the numbers to understand the way of things.

On the edge of every winter, in spring or in fall, for most of the last many years now Heff makes it his business to fly back here. He has his roots and origins to consider, the places he came from in Detroit, the old house in the old neighborhood just a block away from the Hackett Funeral Home and Holy Redeemer Church. He has graves to visit at the cemetery and a friend on the south end of a lake up north. Sometimes he rents a car in Detroit; others he gets a connecting flight and I pick him up at the airport in Pellston. Either way, we have a few days to visit, to cook up some good meals and share new work and carry on about our plans for whatever is left to us of time.

Chapter Six

This Is Just to Say

(On William Carlos Williams)

What drew me to the poems of William Carlos Williams was the unadorned thing-i-ness of them—the sense they seemed determined to affirm that all the poet had to provide was reliable witness to the world in real time—to say what it was he heard or saw without one extra syllable, to record the moment, the happenstance, the instant when the poet's scrutiny turned its focus on one thing instead of another. Thus the cinematic, frame-by-frame, light-beam-of-the-artist's-eye intensity of them, as they made their quite convincing case for Williams's dictum: "no ideas but in things."

THIS IS JUST TO SAY

I have eaten
the plums
that were in
the icebox

and which
you were probably
saving for breakfast

Forgive me
they were delicious
so sweet
and so cold[1]

Here was an American poet at work in the American
century, enamored of American idioms, unencumbered by
the old forms and formalities of Europe, his lexicon tied to
the mundane traffic of talk among everyday citizens, lovers,
husbands, and wives, no references required, traveling light
through the world of things.

What drew me to Williams as a man, and as paradigm for
the writerly life I was trying in my twenties to establish, was
the hyphenated life he had lived quite successfully as a full-
time physician in a small town in New Jersey and a full-time
poet and writer in his correspondences with Pound and his
weekends in New York. Not two things half way, but both
things to the full—he was a good doctor and a real poet.

The life he led out of the clapboard manse at 9 Ridge
Road on a corner lot in Rutherford, New Jersey, seemed like
the life I was bound to lead from the corner of Liberty Boulevard and East Street in Milford, Michigan. Like his house,
my house was built in the late nineteenth century, with high
ceilings and tall drafty windows and fieldstone foundations
and lilacs and forsythia all around. It was a house built in an
age of parlors and birthing rooms—when births and deaths,
courtships and christenings, marriages and illnesses, wakes
and burials were all conducted under the one roof of the
family residence. All of life's one-off events: the baptisms,
nuptials, funerals, were done in big old homes with airy
rooms and elms and oak trees lining the city lots of turn of
the century towns like ours.

Like his, mine was just down the street from the Presbyterian church and the larger traffic of merchants and
shopkeepers. And just as his home included his offices and

examination rooms, mine was next door to my funeral home with its parlors and embalming room, caskets display and coffee lounges.

And like his schedule my schedule was circumscribed by the contingencies of life and death among my neighbors and acquaintances: whatever I wrote, I wrote before or after I'd taken care of whatever disasters or perils presented themselves.

He had a small room on the third floor of his house. I have a room at the front end of mine. Poetry was portable, the line replaying itself in the ears' auditorium until the life of duty and detail yielded the time it took to write things down.

The sense was always evident in Williams's work that poetry was a catch-as-catch-can art: made out of the vigils we keep, the watching and waiting that we do on the lives of people who shared place and time and circumstance with us, and that ours is only to keep the record straight.

THE YOUNG HOUSEWIFE

At ten A.M. the young housewife
moves about in negligee behind
the wooden walls of her husband's house.
I pass solitary in my car.

Then again she comes to the curb
to call the ice-man, fish-man, and stands
shy, uncorseted, tucking in
stray ends of hair, and I compare her
to a fallen leaf.

The noiseless wheels of my car
rush with a crackling sound over
dried leaves as I bow and pass smiling.[2]

This rich internal life, lived out in the confines of his small town in the East, full of observed things, illumined moments, proximate if yet-to-be-connected things, seemed like the life I'd been called to lead on my corner of a small town in the upper Midwest. In America, I thought, we can reinvent ourselves and everything, everything, if only we keep our eyes peeled, ears to the ground, hands at the ready.

> I will teach you my townspeople
> how to perform a funeral—
> for you have it over a troop
> of artists—
> unless one should scour the world—
> you have the ground sense necessary.[3]

I encountered Dr. Williams's guidance on obsequies, a poem he called "Tract," the year before I finished mortuary school.

I was twenty-five. He'd been dead ten years. And truth be told, I thought it pushing the professional envelope some, as if I'd written a poem on pediatrics, to wit:

> I will tell you my townspeople
> How to perform a tonsillectomy!

At first I mistook his title's meaning—thinking he meant it only as "preachment" like the pamphleteering Jehovah's Witnesses did on subjects related to our salvation. But the straightforward, dirge like "ground sense" of the thing— its obsession with the conveyance of the corpse, the hearse and how it ought be outfitted—led me toward the middle English etymology of "tractor" and "plot of ground" that must be "drawn over, dragged," prepared for planting. His counsel has kept me rapt and attentive to its detail all the years—going on forty now—since I became the undertaker in this town.

See! the hearse leads.
I begin with a design for a hearse.
For Christ's sake not black—
nor white either—and not polished!
Let it be weathered—like a farm wagon—
with gilt wheels (this could be
applied fresh at small expense)
or no wheels at all:
a rough dray to drag over the ground.

Knock the glass out!
My God—glass, my townspeople!
For what purpose? Is it for the dead
to look out or for us to see
how well he is housed or to see
the flowers or the lack of them—
or what?
To keep the rain and snow from him?
He will have a heavier rain soon:
pebbles and dirt and what not.
Let there be no glass—
and no upholstery, phew!
and no little brass rollers
and small easy wheels on the bottom—
my townspeople what are you thinking of?

A rough plain hearse then
with gilt wheels and no top at all.
On this the coffin lies
by its own weight.

No wreaths please—
especially no hot house flowers.
Some common memento is better,
something he prized and is known by:
his old clothes—a few books perhaps—

God knows what! You realize
how we are about these things
my townspeople—
something will be found—anything
even flowers if he had come to that.
So much for the hearse.

For heaven's sake though see to the driver!
Take off the silk hat! In fact
that's no place at all for him—
up there unceremoniously
dragging our friend out to his own dignity!
Bring him down—bring him down!
Low and inconspicuous! I'd not have him ride
on the wagon at all—damn him—
the undertaker's understrapper!
Let him hold the reins
and walk at the side
and inconspicuously too!

Then briefly as to yourselves:
Walk behind—as they do in France,
seventh class, or if you ride
Hell take curtains! Go with some show
of inconvenience; sit openly—
to the weather as to grief.
Or do you think you can shut grief in?
What—from us? We who have perhaps
nothing to lose? Share with us
share with us—it will be money
in your pockets.

Go now
I think you are ready.[4]

Of course, a good funeral, I had come to know is more
than the livery and the gilded wheels. More than the glass

or lack of it, and sometimes I wondered if the good doctor's constant focus on the thing itself, to borrow Wallace Stevens's construction, obscured our further meditations on the "idea of the thing." His "Tract" seemed focused on the fashions at the expense of something fundamental. Still, whereas I loved Emily Dickinson for the essential weightedness of her notions:

> After great pain, a formal feeling comes —
> The Nerves sit ceremonious, like Tombs —
> The stiff Heart questions 'was it He, that bore,'
> And 'Yesterday, or Centuries before'?
>
> The Feet, mechanical, go round —
> A Wooden way
> Of Ground, or Air, or Ought —
> Regardless grown,
> A Quartz contentment, like a stone —
>
> This is the Hour of Lead —
> Remembered, if outlived,
> As Freezing persons, recollect the Snow —
> First—Chill—then Stupor—then the letting go—[5]

I loved Williams for the way he asserted meaning in the meaningless:

> so much depends
> upon
>
> a red wheel
> barrow
>
> glazed with rain
> water
>
> beside the white
> chickens.[6]

These twenty-two syllables, these sixteen words, divided into their 4x4 stanzas, four couplets, with their thumping two-count end words, in which, as in Beckett, "nothing happens," "The Red Wheelbarrow" had me stumped for years. As with so many mysteries, I followed Montaigne, and tried to resolve it in a correspondence—as if addressing the good doctor, though dead with years, might, through the alchemy of the language that we both believed in, make itself plain to me. And so I wrote him:

Doctor Williams,

This is just to say I never really got it—that part about so much depending upon a red wheel barrow, etcetera: the glaze of rain water, the white chickens—a fetching mystery, but a mystery nonetheless. I was young when I first encountered it. I counted everything, examined the pattern of stressed and unstressed syllables, after a while just let it be: a little chaser for that one about the plums and the icebox and pleading forgiveness for having eaten them which, needless to say, I took to heart quite readily. I'd give out with bits and pieces of your poems, now and then, to win the attentions of comely girls, some of who actually seemed to understand.

But things happen. The ante gets irretrievably upped by life as we come to know it. Things happen, as you know yourself, without rhyme or reason.

One winter we had two boys go through the ice on the river that runs through town, two brothers, not twins but near enough. The pair of them fit side by side, the older boy's arm around the younger one's shoulder, decked out in their OshKosh B'Gosh bib overall jeans their mother had mail-ordered for them for Christmas.

Six and four, or seven and five? Either way, they both fit inside the one coffin I could not charge their father for.

I remember standing beside that box in the little parlor, those poor hollow parents, holding each other upright, her god-awful sobs, low and animal, and me there with them for what we call, in my line of work, the first viewing. I was not yet thirty and thought I'd seen everything—as if seeing one was seeing all.

And I turned to look out the window on the east side of the parlor into the grey mid-December light, the bald trees up and down East Street, on Liberty the daily traffic undisturbed, the Presbyterian bells on the corner ringing the quarter hour, the shops and cafes and bars on the main drag doing business, and I was searching, Doctor, I remember these more than forty years since, looking out over my corner lots, searching for something, anything to let my gaze seize upon, upon which everything could be said to depend because looking back into the space I was occupying, that moment, with those damaged parents and those drowned little boys, so sweet, so cold, was, as you know yourself, Doctor, impossible.

So this is just to say I know you stood with ruined parents too. And there were things that took your breath away and turned your gaze out of the office windows on your corner of Ridge Road in Rutherford, out across the lawn and gardens, out into the backyard and the old garage where, thanks be to Whoever's in Charge Here, there were the chickens and the wheelbarrow and the rainwater's glaze in which your rheumy eyes found, if neither rhyme nor reason, still momentary repose. For which, I suppose you gave some thanks, for the gaze diverted, the attention turned, the horrible mystery redeemed by some "things." So let me finish with a word of thanks, in the form of a poem I made years ago as a new year's resolution—not the calendar year, but my personal year, my birthday.

Repose,
T. Lynch

REFUSING AT FIFTY-TWO TO WRITE SONNETS

It came to him that he could nearly count
How many Octobers he had left to him
In increments of ten or, say, eleven
Thus: sixty-three, seventy-four, eighty-five.

He couldn't see himself at ninety-six —
Humanity's advances notwithstanding
In health-care, self-help, or New-Age regimens —
What with his habits and family history,
The end he thought is nearer than you think.

The future, thus confined to its contingencies,
The present moment opens like a gift:
The balding month, the grey week, the blue morning,
The hour's routine, the minute's passing glance —
All seem like godsends now. And what to make of this?
At the end the word that comes to him is Thanks.[7]

Poets, Popes, and Laureates

(On Carol Ann Duffy)

I met Carol Ann Duffy in a bar on the south bank of the Thames, in November more than twenty years ago.

I want that to sound cinematic, gauzy, and memorable because it was and remains, in my memory, like an old movie, in black and white, vintage Hollywood, the end of a day that has replayed itself in my memory many times.

I had just done a reading at the South Bank Centre with Jackie Kay, Ms. Duffy's companion then and country-woman. I was surrounded by Scots and Welsh, Irish and English poets, East Indians and Pakistanis, a novelist from Melbourne, a South African writer, all of whose talk and idiomatic nuances were, quite literally, music to my ears.

> At the turn of the river the language changes,
> a different babble, even a different name
> for the same river. Water crosses the border,
> translates itself, but words stumble, fall back,
> and there, nailed to a tree, is proof. A sign
>
> in a new language brash on a tree. A bird
> not seen before, singing on a branch. A woman

on the path by the river, repeating a strange sound
to clue the bird's song and ask for its name, after.
She kneels for a red flower, picks it, later
will press it carefully between the pages of a book.[1]

Ms. Duffy's early poem, "River," speaks to language's
many tributaries and currents. And to be sure, meeting her
there at the South Bank Centre, in the city where so many
different tongues become, as it were, confluent, was, in my
memory of it, deeply spiritual.

I'd been in the market for a religious experience and
had just returned, but days before, from a brief off-season
pilgrimage to Iona in the Hebrides, haunt of the great
sixth-century saint, Columba, or Columcille, the "dove of
the church" in the English of it.

A native of Donegal, Columba was born of royalty and
raised by a priest who taught him to read the Psalms. There
had been the usual signs of sanctity. He cursed a man to
death once and once turned spring water into wine. It was
certain he would have an important future. Later he studied
with St. Finnian, whose psalter he copied and was going to
keep until Finnian found out and objected. The case came
before the high king, Diarmuid who ruled famously: "to
every cow her calf, to every book its copy."

Columba, apparently not free of character flaws, returned
the psalter but went to war with Diarmuid and defeated him
in a battle in which hundreds died. In penance for which
bloodletting, Columba exiled himself from Ireland and
vowed to convert as many pagans as men who died in the
battle. The Picts of Scotland seemed the handiest pagans,
so in a coracle with twelve kinsmen, he sailed off the north
coast of Ireland in 563. He went from island to island until
he could no longer see, through the fog and sea mists, the
coast of his beloved Ulster so that his exile would be truly
penitential. He came ashore in a small bay on the west side

of Iona and looking back into the fog, saw nothing and so decided to stay.

I'd always wanted to see this place.

The long train ride north to Glasgow, thence to Oban, felt to me like pilgrimage. I went without a plan or reservation, drawn to it by an aching to be there. In Oban late at night, I took a room overlooking the esplanade, and in the morning made the first boat to the Isle of Mull, thence by bus to Fionnphort on the far side of Mull and finally, by smaller ferry, across the mile-wide sound, to the tiny treeless island of the saint.

It was noonish in a place where the light would only last until four o'clock that late in the year. The hotels were shuttered for the season. I was directed to a woman who operated a guesthouse near the pier. I paid her and went out to make what I could of the daylight.

I walked out to the small bay where the saint had first landed centuries before. I met no one on the road and saw no one in the fields, only the cattle with their abundant horns. When I got to the sea's edge I sat among the large rocks that littered the deserted strand, looking south and west the way the saint was said to have looked. I was alone in the off season, on an island in the sea, ready and willing and eager for the voice of God.

The tide surged, gulls circled overhead, the gray light of the sun behind the clouds was cold.

Presently in my vigil I saw the figure of a man approaching and assumed he would, in keeping with the international custom among spiritual tourists, walk his own path, leaving me to mine and to my soul's own reveries.

On spying me, however, the man adjusted the angle of his ambulation so as to arrive in no time with a hearty "hello there" in an accent I took to be East Anglian. He had the fleshy face of a tenor chorister or altar boy and the aspect of someone running for public office.

In short order and without solicitation, I was possessed of the man's particulars:

He was thirty, the son of Irish parents who'd emigrated to England, he was a priest, on leave from parish work in a suburb of Glasgow where he'd been the curate for a year, sent to Iona by his bishop for a little rest, "you know, to recharge the batteries, you know!" He did not elaborate on the nature of his "fatigue."

He proffered his right hand. "Fr. Peter."

"Lynch," I said, "Thomas Lynch."

"May I take from your name you are a coreligionist?"

Before I could answer, he carried on. He was so glad to find another Catholic here. He'd been staying at the Abbey for a fortnight now among an array of Anglicans and Presbyterians, Baptists and Wesleyans.

"All very nice, you know, but not the same."

Fr. Peter was feeling a little banished to the hinterlands.

"And what brings you to Iona?" the priest queried me.

I told him that I'd just felt drawn to see the place; that my life had achieved of late an unaccustomed calm for which I was, here in the moment, filled with thanks.

Mostly I told him, I was thankful for the lives of my sons and my daughter and the love of the woman I'd married just months before, after years of consort, second-guessing and procrastination.

I was grateful for her beauty and good counsel and the peace she had brought to our household where, at the moment and thousands of miles away, she was tending to the welfare of her stepchildren.

The cleric, I could see, was calculating.

"Did your first wife die? The mother of your children?"

His question caught me by surprise.

"No, oh, no, thanks be to God . . . divorced. We were divorced. Years ago now."

"And was the original marriage annulled, then?"

"No," I told him. "I could never bring myself to turn over to men who had never been married the job of deciding if my former spouse and I had been."

"Well, you know, the church still recognizes your first marriage as valid and binding."

By the time it was over, I told the man, it was completely invalid, a blight on my children, my former spouse and me hobbled with mistrust and mutual contempt.

"You know of course that as far as the church is concerned you're living in adultery with this other woman."

Whereupon I found myself looking around the beach for a stone or a plank of driftwood or something with which to bang the man at the place on his face from which the odious pronouncements were issuing forth.

Something my father used to always say about there being no shortage of certain body parts in the world came into mind just then.

"Bugger off, Peter, you unsufferable asshole."

He stood up from the rock he'd seated himself upon, shocked, blushing, muttering something about not blaming the messenger, clearly unpracticed at being told what to do. I stared into the space between my feet and could feel the fist forming with which to smite him and the coincident urge to do the needful thing over and over until he was silenced.

To every cow its calf, I told myself; to every asshole its thumping. I stood up straight and took a step in his direction. He turned on his heel and ran off briskly, blathering on about the eyes of the church.

After a dark night on the island, I returned, by ferryboat and hired car, train and night bus, to London. A long journey made sour by a surly churchman.

Possibly this is why, after reading with Jackie Kay, and feeling the wash of welcome and thanksgiving in every version of the English language, and being ushered into an informal audience with a poet whose work I knew before I knew her, possibly this is why it felt holy when I first met Carol Ann Duffy.

Or was it because she bore more than a passing semblance to the cherubic priest I'd lately tangled with on Iona? But whereas his gob oozed orthodoxy and exclusion, Carol Ann seemed lighthearted and luminous, priestly and druidic as if she could, by dint of will, command the weather and the elements.

And in all the years since then, whenever I have encountered Ms. Duffy, this richly liturgical air she has about her grows more manifest.

When we read together in Galway in the middle '90s, and she was traveling with her mother and her then toddling daughter, she seemed to have come into her strength.

All the more so in the noughties when we shared a stage in Newcastle West and her daughter had grown into a sparkling girl and Carol Ann on the brink of her laureateship seemed ready to rise to the occasion. And last winter in Michigan, where we'd coaxed her to come to lecture and read to students—the discernably homiletic aspect of her work was evident.

> After I learned to transubstantiate
> unleavened bread
> into the sacred host
>
> and swung the burning frankincense
> till blue-green snakes of smoke
> coiled round the hem of my robe

The priestly magic of transubstantiation—turning one thing into another, is after all the stuff of poetry.

The first female laureate, like the first female pope, can be forgiven for noticing the trappings of office.

and swayed through those fervent crowds,
high up in a papal chair,
blessing and blessing the air,

nearer to heaven
than cardinals, archbishops, bishops, priests,
being Vicar of Rome,

having made the Vatican my home,
like the best of men,
in nomine patris et filii et spiritus sancti, amen,

but twice as virtuous as them,
I came to believe
that I did not believe a word,[2]

Like Carol Ann I've found that Catholicism has been too often at odds with catholicity. Membership in the universal, all embracing church of humanity seems too often at odds with the church such as we've come to know it—an institution of feckless Fr. Peters and his well heeled up-line, a clericalism which seeks to keep the reverend clergy in charge of God's laws.

The church triumphant has become, late in one millennium and early in another, most famous for the rape of children and the coddling of pederasts and other criminals and the longstanding devaluation of women's lives. It makes of the woman who has given her life, selflessly, to the care of my children and the repair of my soul, an adultress.

It would make of Ms. Duffy, if she gave a rap, a deeply "disordered" sinner. It would withhold communion from politicos, poets, and pilgrims like me, all in the name of Holy Mother the Church, an institution which, in the hands of the red cassocked and ermine-clad dandies that man its

ramparts, has become more abusive than holy of late. All the
same, the language of creation is made in the flesh
    so I tell you now, (Carol Ann continues)

        so I tell you now
        daughters or brides of the Lord,
        that the closest I felt

        to the power of God
        was the sense of a hand
        lifting me, flinging me down,

        lifting me, flinging me down,
        as my baby pushed out
        from between my legs

        where I lay in the road
        in my miracle,
        not a man or a pope at all.[3]

This remarkable declarative sentence, "Pope Joan" from
Carol Ann's collection, *The World's Wife*, reveals itself over
ten tercets giving voice to a cross-dressing woman who
passed for a pope and was never revealed, never unveiled,
until her creative miracle was made manifest.

For Ms. Duffy as for Beckett, "all poetry is prayer." She
achieves what Beckett also admired, the mind that has raised
itself to the "grace of humility"—as woman, as mother, as
poet she bides near enough to the power of God embodied.

Fr. Peter and the mitered old men around Peter's throne
seem clueless as to the lives of women. They are flummoxed
by thoughts of female priesthood or married clergy or gay
clergy or poets who transfigure ordinary words into Eucha-
ristic feasts, who conjure images of God's grandeur and who
live out the Beatitudes in the flesh.

What if a pope and his entourage of crosiered posers were to abdicate the throne of Peter in favor of exile and penance, leaving the holy mother, the church, in the hands of fierce poets and wayfarers like Columba or Carol Ann? How many of the devoutly lapsed would be restored to faith by such acts of God?

Chapter Eight

Haunts

(On Michael Donaghy)

I first met Michael Donaghy in 1991. He was a force of nature with his toothy grin, garrulousness, fierce intellect, and prepossession.

"'I was the handsomest boy at school,' he'll say, straight-faced at fifty," Michael says of his dead father conjured in his poem, "Caliban's Books." He is retelling the story of how his father was chosen for the school play by Mr. Quinn. And how the father's books and marginalia haunt him still.

When Michael died in 2004, too soon, too cruelly, too suddenly at fifty, he was among the handsomest boys in that singing school of poets and musicians that were his life and times in the UK and Ireland, where he was most admired among his fellow choristers.

It was a Sunday afternoon I met him, in mid-November more than a quarter century ago, in the kitchen of the home he kept in North London with his partner, Maddy Paxman. It was one of those gatherings for no apparent reason, a feast for no particular saint or season, a Sunday among still youngish poets then: Ruth Padel and Vicki Feaver, Don Paterson and Jo Shapcott, Sean O'Brien, Maurice Riordan, Wendy Cope, and Matthew Sweeney with whom I'd come, the visiting Yank on his first book's tour into the literary salons of the language's capital. We were all, I think, still finding our ways, some books in the stalls, some works in progress. All of us making the usual rounds of readings and launches, workshops and round tables. The spread of cheeses and crackers, wines and spirits, easy talk and lots of laughter.

And because Michael was himself a hyphenated man—American by birth, Irish by tribe, and English by pursuit of the woman he loved—and because it was his nature to welcome, he welcomed me into his home with the great grinning visage, the play in his eyes and the torrent of hurried speech that always issued forth from him, a river's low drone of constantly flowing talk. He was, as the bromide holds, an easy man to like.

I'd meet up with Michael in the years to come in England and Ireland, by design or happenstance. In the spring of '97 we both had duties at the Cúirt Festival in Galway. I was launching a book of essays. He was giving out with his poems: the famous "Machines" and "Shibboleth," those Bronx and Chicago pieces from *O'Ryan's Belt*: "The Hunter's Purse," "A Repertoire," "A Reprieve."

Neither of us were the main event, which was dominated by Seamus Heaney that year, home to the locals with his Nobel Prize. Between duties, we lesser luminaries basked in the city of the tribes. Michael shopped the traditional music shops and record stalls and gave me guidance on the great Clare fiddlers. We shopped at Kennys Bookshop and Charlie Byrne's. We were all installed in the Atlanta Hotel where every night the bar stayed opened late for the literati and their entourages. One morning, free of obligations, I drove him and Maddy and their not-quite toddling boy Ruairi out to Yeats's tower at Thoor Ballylee, each of us giving out with bits and pieces of the great man's poems, Maddy with the baby rolling their eyes and smiling in the rearview mirror.

I, the poet William Yeats,
With old mill boards and sea-green slates
And smithy work from the Gort forge
Restored this tower for my wife George;
And may these characters remain
When all is ruin once again.[1]

We speculated as to what were the odds that Yeats would marry a woman, if not for her towering good looks—not often a thing Mrs. Yeats was accused of—then for the rhyme he could make of her name with "Gort forge." Michael thought it would be worth the nuptials. He had the musician's ear for the acoustics of language.

October that same year we read together with the Australian master, Les Murray, at the Cheltenham Festival in the great town hall on Imperial Square, all of us kept at the Queens Hotel. I was reading from a new book of essays and he was trying out the poems that would become, in a few short years, his prize-winning collection, *Conjure*. They were full of ghosts, these poems, disembodied voices, apparitions, hauntings. The body and the soul of things always struggling toward a kind of connection: part liturgy, part incantation, he said them out like plain chants of sacred texts he'd long ago learned off by heart. It's where I first heard him recite his poem "Reprimands," which he introduced with a nod to the Gospel of John, those verses in the twentieth chapter where Doubting Thomas is confronted by the risen Christ, who tenders his wounds for the apostle's scrutiny.

Then saith he to Thomas, Reach hither thy finger, and behold my hands; and reach hither thy hand, and thrust it into my side: and be not faithless, but believing.
And Thomas answered and said unto him, My Lord and my God.
Jesus saith unto him, Thomas, because thou hast seen me,

thou hast believed: blessed are they that have not seen, and
yet have believed.

(John 20:27–29 KJV)

In every painting the doubter's finger is poised to touch
the blooded palm of the Savior's hand or trembles toward
the wound in the Savior's side. The poem is a meditation on
faith and faithlessness, doubt and wonder, the predicament
of being "of two minds," twinned, caught between blind
trust and overthinking, like all of Donaghy, a feast for the
ears:

> We fell out of love as toddlers fall
> glancing down, distracted, at their feet,
> as the pianist in the concert hall
> betrays her hands to thought and adds an extra beat—
> The thought vertiginous. The reprimand.
> It fells the bee mid-flight. It made me stall
> before a holy water font in Rome
> half afraid that if I dipped my hand
> I'd find the water's surface hard as stone
> And—this you'd never understand—
> half afraid to leave the thing alone.
> For I'd been taught that Jesus walked the sea
> and came to Peter three leagues out of port.
> Said Peter *Bid me to come unto thee*
> and strode on faith dryfoot until he thought . . .
> and thinking, sank. I'd never learnt to swim
> but I'd seen insects skim across a pond
> and I'd seen glasses filled above the brim.
> Some firm conviction keeps a raindrop round.
> What kept me rigid as a mannequin?[2]

By this time in his all too brief career, Michael was
declaiming his poems from memory. So thoroughly and
so seamlessly wrought by the time they saw the light of

day in some good journal's ink, these pieces had inhabited him like language itself, a sort of second tongue that made sense of things for which ordinary talk was unequipped. It was something that he came to by a little accident—this performance of his work—when he left his books and papers on a train, hurrying to a reading in some midlands village.

He found his compositions were not only memorable, they were memorizable in the best of the bardic tradition to which Michael claimed his own direct lineage—that the performance of a poem, the giving it out loud in its maker's voice, was part of an oral tradition before it was part of a literary one.

Poets, he knew from his own studies, were the original newscasters of the world, making their way from parish to parish bringing news of the former place to the current one: Who stole who's cow? Who slept with who's daughter? Which king's kinsman vanquished the others?

Long before it was a written and read thing, poetry was a heard and a said thing, notable for its acoustic cues and musicality, as often as not with accompaniment—some drummer or whistler or strummer of tunes—and the poet was first of all the bringer of news and the purveyor of truths, the caster of spells and powerful medicines known only to them. Michael saw himself as part of this long tradition, this stewardship of sound and sense that turns word works loose into the world.

Having rejected the more comfortable life he might have had in his home country, tutoring graduate students in some MFA program—a kind of pyramid scheme or personality cult by which the culture gets its art like clean drinking water and good infrastructure, and the poets get good pensions and dental coverage; having rather followed his heart and his beloved to England in 1985, he had claimed the right to worship openly at the altar of language, to pursue the gift of tongues he proclaims in "Pentecost."

The neighbours hammered on the walls all night,
Outraged by the noise we made in bed.
Still we kept it up until by first light
We'd said everything that could be said.

Undaunted, we began to mewl and roar
As if desire had stripped itself of words.
Remember when we made those sounds before?
When we built a tower heavenwards
They were our reward for blasphemy.
And then again, two thousand years ago,
We huddled in a room in Galilee
Speaking languages we didn't know,
While amethyst uraeuses of flame
Hissed above us. We recalled the tower
And the tongues. We knew this was the same,
But love had turned the curse into a power.

See? It's something that we've always known:
Though we command the language of desire,
The voice of ecstasy is not our own.
We long to lose ourselves amid the choir
Of the salmon twilight and the mackerel sky,
The very air we take into our lungs,
And the rhododendron's cry.

And when you lick the sweat along my thigh,
Dearest, we renew the gift of tongues.[3]

This easy melding of the sacred and the sensual, the holy and the happy flesh of things is signature Donaghy.

And seeing him lean in toward the microphone, that autumn afternoon in Cheltenham, close his eyes as if reimagining the way the poem first made itself apparent to him; he'd cock his ear into the air and begin, the words becoming flesh in the echo chamber sounding box of his voice, a pied piper in his jeans and tweedy coat.

His faith in language—the sense one gets in hearing his poems that the right word will present itself if the poet just keeps his ears properly tuned to the voices he is haunted by: the lovers, the dead parents and poets, the son he conjures in the future, all the elegant ghosts he has heard humming from the shelves at the public library—it is not scholarship. It is immersion—the grasp and hold and touch by which the lexicon binds us, like baptismal waters, to its magic and powers. We needn't overthink it or over study: the world of words operates as pure metaphor that connects seemingly unrelated things through rhyme and verse and etymologies, the infinite confluence of meanings. If we look too closely, we are likely to falter, whereas if we trust in language it keeps us all afloat:

We fell out of love and nearly drowned.
The very wordlessness all lovers want
to feel beneath their feet like solid ground
dissolved to silences no human shout
could ripple—

                    like the surface of that font
when other voices, tourist and devout,
grew still, and someone whispered by my side
O ye of little faith—and shallow doubt—
choose here to wet that hand or stand aside.
No one was there. But I could tell that tone.
I heard his ancient apostolic voice
this evening when I went to lift the phone
to tell you this—and froze. The reprimand.
For once, in two minds, Thomas made the choice
to bless and wet with blood his faithless hand.[4]

I remember going off with him afterward, to the May-flower Restaurant, the two of us guests of bookish and generous locals, for a feast of Peking duck and drinks and more good talk, walking back the high street seeing ourselves, well feted, well fed, like blurry goblins in the shop front windows.

It was, I think, the following summer I found myself back in London again and hearing that I was in town with my own son, Michael called to see if we'd like a tour of Highgate Cemetery. He had worked there as a tour guide in the years before he won all the prizes and the regard of his peers.

He brought his son, just going on two, in one of those backpacks parents use. My own son, Michael, was twenty that year. He was just going into mortuary school, to join me in our family undertaking. We walked among the obelisks and statuary, the tombs and mausoleums of notables and negligibles. I have a photo of my son, Michael, and Michael and his Ruairi, all posing with the stone head of Karl Marx, everyone grinning in the necropolis, sons haunted by fathers, fathers haunted by sons, trying to cipher life's most vexing riddle.

Poets are among the most happily haunted sorts and Irish poets are happier still to be inundated with the voices of those gone—parents and old publicans, lovers and beloveds, rhymers and reasoners like ourselves, constantly trying the shibboleths, errata and conjurings.

ACT 3, SCENE 2:

Be not afeard. The isle is full of noises,
Sounds, and sweet airs that give delight and hurt not.
Sometimes a thousand twangling instruments
Will hum about mine ears; and sometime voices

So Shakespeare gives the wild Caliban—the figure Donaghy's father played at age 14—to say in his famous *Tempest* speech, Act 3, Scene 2.

The sounds and sweet airs, the noises and voices that wake us from our sleep are not meant to frighten, but to encourage and console, to embolden with faith in the gift of tongues.

The last time I heard him read, Michael closed with his poem "Haunts," one long timeless loop of a sentence whereby the child becomes the father of the man, each eventually consoling the other with the faith that soothes all fears. It is a faith that Donaghy practiced in abundance, the sense that the spirit of the language so abided in him that he could make lasting and memorable sense of anything, as proof of which his poems outlive him. There is, in this yuletide meditation, something of the apparition of the risen Christ in the upper room among the shaken disciples, the transfigured, wounded, broken, and restored beloved:

HAUNTS

Don't be afraid, old son, it's only me,
though not as I've appeared before,
on the battlements of your signature,
or margin of a book you can't throw out,
or darkened shop front where your face
first shocks itself into a mask of mine,
but here, alive, one Christmas long ago
when you were three, upstairs, asleep,
and haunting *me* because I conjured you
the way that child you were would cry out
waking in the dark, and when you spoke
in no child's voice but out of radio silence,
the hall clock ticking like a radar blip,
a bottle breaking faintly streets away,
you said, as I say now, *Don't be afraid.*[5]

Chapter Nine

An Eye for an Eyeness

(On the Lord's Prayer)

And forgive us, we plead, forgive us our trespasses, still red in tooth and claw, still huffing and puffing from the latest pillage or deceit—as we forgive those who trespass against us. This repentant cousin of the Golden Rule begs Whomever's in Charge Here to do unto us as we do unto others for the sins or savageries or slights between us.

Of course, this runs contrary to our vengeful natures, which prefer to nurse our hurts and steep our grievances, blunting them into blade or cudgel, the better to bludgeon or cut the pound of recompense. We both want and do not want, in the marketplace of ethics, whatever we have coming to us: the pound of flesh, or perpetual perdition.

We make our case as we are instructed by our brother and homilist, the Nazarene, to Our Father in Heaven, and by so doing make a case for our kinship with God. We are all children of the same creation, heirs to the one crown, peers in the kingdom that we pray will come, pilgrims on a journey in search of home.

And what head of household, what loving parent, wanting a peaceable kingdom among the wards and protégés, wouldn't teach them to pray for such forbearance, such tolerance of imperfections, such forgiveness? Love one another, we will elsewhere be counseled, as I have loved you.

It sounds like a father or a mother, clement and kindly, all comfort and sweet coaxing—the kind of family we'd all want to come from, where no one drank too much or ever got cranky or mouthy, abusive or divorced, and the wee freckle-faced princes and princesses all got along instead of daily trying to dismember each other in pursuit of their own pure animal wants.

My mother taught us to say our prayers and taught my children before she died. The Hail Marys and Glory Bes, Our Fathers and Apostles' Creed, which were comingled in a kind of holy medley to become, with thumbs and forefingers working the beads, the joyful and sorrowful mysteries. The keeping track of trespasses we came by naturally, as a kind of coin of the realm in the marketplace of our holy family.

We said prayers before meals and journeys, the Angel of God at bedtime, some holy aubade at waking, and throughout the day deployed a series of "ejaculations"—quick little arrows of prayer for specific targets: "Baby Jesus, lost and found." "Eternal rest grant unto them, and rest in peace." And the all-purpose evocation, "Thanks be to God."

Our tribal dialect was peppered with bromides and medicines, "the Lord have mercy on 'em" and "saints be praised," and for the more formal occasions a "let us pray" that almost always included a recitation of The Lord's Prayer, cut into the stone of the Sermon on the Mount in the red letter discourse of Matthew's Gospel.

Our tribe—my family of origin—did not read the Bible. We got it in doses, daily or weekly, from a priest bound by the lectionary to give us bits and pieces in collects, Epistles, Gospels and graduals, which, along with Confiteor and Kyrie, formed the front-loaded, word-rich portion of the Tridentine Mass. These were followed by sacred table work and common feed, to wit laving and consecration,

Communion, thanksgiving and benediction. On Sundays, it'd all be seasoned with some lackluster homiletics—linked haphazardly to the Scriptures of the day. These liturgies were labor intensive, heavy on costume and stagecraft, holy theater. Possibly this is why few priests put much time into preaching, preferring, as the writing workshops say, "to show rather than to tell."

Still, we knew the stories: Eden and the apple, the murderous brother, the prodigal and good whore, floods and leviathans; we knew mangers and magi, scribes and Pharisees and repentant thieves. I remember my excitement, the first time I heard about the woman washing the Savior's feet with her tears, wiping them with her long hair, and anointing them with perfume. My father, a local undertaker, was especially fond of Joseph of Arimathea and his sidekick, Nicodemus, who'd bargained with Pilate for the corpse of Christ and tended to the burial in Joseph's own tomb, newly hewn from rock, "in keeping with the customs of the Jews."

Sex and the dead, a good book, indeed!

And though we had a Bible at home—an old counter-Reformation, Douay-Rheims translation from the Latin Vulgate of St. Jerome's fourth-century text—we rarely read the thing. It was a holy knick-knack, like the statue of the Blessed Mother, the picture of the Sacred Heart, the table-top manger scene that came out for Christmas, the crucifixes over each of our beds, the holy water font at the front door—all designed to suit our daily praxis. We kept the fasts and abstinences of Lent and Advent along with whatever novena was in fashion and most likely to inure to our spiritual betterments. We abstained from meat on Friday, confessed our sins on Saturday, kept holy the Sabbath, such as we knew it, and basked in the assurance that ours was the one true faith. Ours was a holy, Roman, Irish-American, post-war-baby-booming, suburban family—sacramental, liturgical, replete with none-too-subtle guilt and shaming, the big magic of transubstantiation, binding and loosing, the true presence, cardinal sins, contrary virtues, states of grace, and the hope for heaven. Litanies and chaplets stood in for Scriptures and hermeneutics.

By twenty I was happily apostate, having come into my disbelief, my devout lapsedness, some few years after puberty when a fellow pilgrim showed me all that she could of the exquisite mysteries of life. If the nuns had been wrong about sex, and they manifestly had been—it was nearer to holiness and, well, rectitude, than not eating meat on Friday—it followed, I reasoned, they were wrong on other things.

"Why do you reason about these things in your hearts?" Jesus asks the naysaying elders in Capernaum, in Mark's telling of the healing of a paralytic (Mark 2 NKJV). They are trying to catch his blaspheming out, in the way we are always conniving against our spiritual betters. I was no different.

The deaths of innocents, the random little disasters that swept young mothers to their dooms in childbirth, their infants to their sudden crib deaths, young lovers to their demises in cars, perfect strangers to their hapless ends, seemed more evidence than anyone should need that whoever is in charge of these matters had a hit-and-miss record on humanity.

I only go to church now for baptisms or weddings or funerals. The mysteries of life, joyous and sorrowful, are regular enough that I count as friends the reverend clergy, whose personal charities and heroics I've been an eyewitness to for many years. But dogma and dicta are at odds with sound reason, and the management class of The Church, all churches, seems uniquely wrongheaded and impressively feckless. What's more, my views on same-sex marriage, the ordination of women, priestly celibacy, and redemptive suffering have rendered me, no doubt, an ex-communicant.

Still, though I neither believe nor belong, nonetheless I behold, in the mysteries of my own experience, a here-again-and-gone-tomorrow sense that Whoever is in Charge Here is certainly not me, and is, furthermore, doing a serviceable job. The sky is not falling. The gladness of creation outshines its griefs. I was and remain, though cranky enough, more grateful than begrudging. Whoever God is, she is—for if not utterly transgendered, God is amiably a cross-dresser who some days sounds like my dead, sainted mother, and on others pretty clearly like my dad—whoever God is, she knows my heart; he holds me close, and hears me often as not when I pray.

Context is everything, a churchman once told me, when, as has been my habit and practice, I'd proffer a contrarian's view of the Scriptures.

"Why," I remember asking him once, on the subject of circumcision as recorded in Genesis 17, "Why didn't they settle on a secret hand-shake or tattoo or tonsure or an ear-ring—something to set the chosen people apart from the pagans—besides lopping the foreskin off of one's manly part? What sort of God goes straight for the genitals?" I can't remember what he told me; it was too late anyway. Foreskins were a moot point among my kinsmen by then.

Though increasingly irreligious, I was observant. I had a kind of religious literacy. I knew the stories and the storytellers, the plots and characters, the dialogues and the narrative arcs.

"Which is easier," Jesus asks the begrudgers, in the corner of the crowded room in Capernaum into which the paralytic has been lowered by four pals from the opened ceiling. Jesus has pronounced his sins forgiven and the scribes and Pharisees know they have him now because only God can forgive sins. The Nazarene had blasphemed.

"Which is easier," he asks them, "to forgive his sins or to say stand and walk?"

It is, of course, a trick question. Because we are all hobbled by the hurts and heartbreaks we can't forgive: those done to us and those done by us. Everyone has a former spouse or estranged child, or lost cause or daylong, lifelong cross, an unholy appetite or unquenchable thirst.

"Your sins are forgiven. Stand and walk," he tells the paralytic, whereupon your suddenly unburdened man rolls up his bed and hastens away, the healing of his body affirming a faith that becomes the healing of his soul.

The Lord's Prayer with its pleadings and beseechings is found in a longer discourse on the nature of grace, gladness, goodness, and law. I think of the fresco by Fra Angelico— the haloed Galileans on sandstone tuffets, the pastel-clad preacher, as latter-day Moses, holding forth. The Sermon on the Mount, as it has come to be called, covers nearly three chapters of Matthew's Gospel, and the directive about how it is we should pray follows close on the heels of the Beatitudes and some explication on the "fulfillments of the law," which Jesus reminds he has come to do. He says some things on murder and trouble with a brother, on adultery and lusting in the heart, on divorce and swearing of oaths and then some further explications of the law.

"You have heard it said," he says to anyone in earshot, "an eye for an eye, a tooth for a tooth. But I tell you, do not resist an evil person. If someone strikes on one cheek, turn the other. If someone sues for your tunic, give him your cloak as well. If someone forces you to go one mile, go with them two."

"You have heard that it was said, 'Love your neighbor and hate your enemy.' But I tell you, love your enemies and pray for those who persecute you." (Matt. 5:43–44 NIV)

It seems these are the new directives upon which a code for good conduct ought to be built: the turned cheek, the coat off your back, the extra mile, returning good for evil. This is the "new deal," the "new testament" where rather than sacrifice, what's called for is mercy.

Still there seems a kind of eye-for-an-eyeness, in the line in the prayer about forgiveness, a tooth-for-toothedness, a quid pro quo: God forgives us only if we forgive our brethren?

This contingent forgiveness is reaffirmed, lest we didn't get it the first time, in the first verse after the prayer is over:

> "For if you forgive other people when they sin against you, your heavenly Father will also forgive you. But if you do not forgive others their sins, your Father will not forgive your sins."
>
> Matt. 6:14–15 NIV

And later in Matthew is the parable of the unforgiving servant: the notion that our forgiveness depends on our willingness to forgive.

Maybe it's the Golden Rule dressed up in its prayerful Sunday best. Central to the case the Our Father makes is that we are in this together; all children of God, the same but different, and that forgiveness is a grace—abundant and undeserved—a gift we likewise give and get, a we program, an inside job, a family business, impossible to accomplish on our own. In order to get it, we must let go.

To get along with our father, our mother in heaven, frazzled as they no doubt are by our wars and distempers, our hardened hearts, our refusal to forgive, forget, our failures to love; to get along with whomever God is, we must, the homilist reminds, somehow get along with one another.

Chapter Ten

Preaching to Bishops

"Preaching to bishops is like farting at skunks," a long-dead churchman told me years ago. "You'll win some battles, but you'll lose the war."

All the more so, no doubt, the higher you go: like crapping at pachyderms, the Lord spare us all. His Holiness, their Eminences and Excellencies: "Don't cross 'em," the curate cautioned me, "those boyos aren't to be tampered with."

The great blessing of my life's work as a funeral director is that it has put me in earshot of the reverend clergy trying to make sense of senseless things as they speak into the gaping maw of the unspeakable: the man who kills his wife, their toy poodle, then himself; a mother who drowns her baby then does her nails; the teenager with the broken heart and loaded pistol, the tumors and emboli, flus and tsunamis, deadly contagions and misadventures—the endless incarnations of the book of Job by which, as no less a magus than Donald Rumsfeld once observed, "stuff happens."

When someone shows up—priest or pastor, rabbi or imam, venerable master or fellow traveler—to stand with the living and the dead, armed with nothing more than a shred of faith and helpful purpose, I know I am witnessing uncommon courage and my perpetually shaken faith is emboldened by theirs.

"Behold, I show you a mystery," they always say, or words to that effect. They are balm and anointing, these men and women of God, frontline infantry and holy corpsmen in the wars between our own worst animas and ourselves. They risk seeming ridiculous to give us a glimpse of the sublime.

Which is why much of the world's ecclesiastical mischief by rear and upper echelon sorts seems so cartoonish, so unseemly, so lacking in gravitas by comparison. Another incident of papal poaching of "traditionalist" Anglicans—to wit, those who are not chuffed at the prospect of female clerics and homosexuals—is but one sup of thin gruel boiled up lately by the hierarchies. Another is the disapprobation of Bishop Burke, late of St. Louis, now installed in a cushy Vatican post, upon Seán Cardinal O'Malley (who took up Bernard Cardinal Law's cross in Boston) over the latter's opening of the church's arms to the corpse of the late Edward Kennedy—a senator and self-confessed sinner of epic proportions—and to his widow and family and leaders of the free world. Then there is its regional, minor league version: The Right Reverend Thomas Tobin's holding forth on the sacramental options open to the late senator's son, Patrick Kennedy, who votes with his caucus on matters of civil law. "Erratic" is the word His Excellency used to describe the congressman's conduct—twisting the prick of insinuation as we Irish-American Catholics so deftly do.

Here in Ireland, the shoes of the fishermen are on the other foot. Coincident with the worst flooding in any memory, the cruel local version of the Great Recession, and nationwide public sector strikes, the report of Judge Yvonne Murphy on priestly abuses in the Dublin Diocese is not so much a reiteration of old news about pedophiles, but rather a stark indictment of the up-line of hierarchs who have colluded with civil authorities to provide cover and protection for such criminals. Bishops, it turns out, behave like "company guys" protecting the interests of the world's oldest merger and acquisition firm from any whiff of scandal. Their calculated malfeasance has done permanent damage to the faithful and to faithful priests who will spend the rest of their lives trying to repair trusts they never had a hand in breaking. The Murphy Report and the stonewalling from Rome and its emissaries have occasioned calls for the removal of the papal nuncio, for the immediate sacking of bishops named in the report, the removal of public schools from diocesan sponsorship, and for the church to be once and forever disentangled from the civic life of an outraged nation.

Back at home, watching the Vatican's inquisition of religious American women for becoming uppity makes many of us who were well schooled in faith and morals by nuns even more devoutly lapsed than we've been for years. Trying to retain the imitation of Christ our faith calls us to whilst removing ourselves from the endless contretemps and imbroglios of the church's princely caste is becoming more the mugs game than ever.

The church is already served by a priesthood of women, gay bishops, and good Catholics who have long ignored the preachments of the old boys on sexual and reproductive matters. To be blind to what is whilst proclaiming what isn't is not faith. It is denial. The church's people have moved along, even if the prelates won't.

Bringing the dead and their families into church is something I've been doing all my life, first with my father, then with my brothers and sisters, now with my sons and nieces and nephews. It is what we've been "called" to do. Not by a voice from on high or a burning bush, but by the voices of our own kind, in the middle of the night, in the middle of dinner, in the middle of otherwise uneventful days. They call for help when there is trouble. And I know when the clergy who meet us in the journey—whether male or female, gay or straight, celibate or sexually active, whether robed in talliths or white chasubles, Brooks Brothers suit or business casual, reciting from Bible or Torah, Koran or Zen koan, with incense, icon, or ancient liturgy—I know they bring a brave and human narrative to bear on the existential questions: Is that all there is? Can it happen to me? Why is it cold? What comes next?

In earshot of such powerful medicines, the high-churchy intrigues and inquisitions, the connivance of bishops and their quibbling seem a waste of God's precious gifts of grace and time.

Chapter Eleven

On Asses

I come by my interests in asses honestly.

A thing my late father used to say applies, to wit: "The thing about asses is everyone's got one." He'd heard this from his father who'd heard it from his father who'd brought it hither from the old country. He'd wink and return to his usual duties. My father was a sober and elegant man, so to hear him on such topics was sufficiently at odds with his usual decorum that it remains lodged in my memory as a thing apart. Opposed on principle to intemperate speech, these constructs were as near as my father would get to bad-mouthing an offensive man, and in truth such reckless- ness never trespassed the gender divide. The asses of women never entered his conversation with his sons. No doubt he admired a well-wrought rump, as we do, but he was scrupu- lous in his prudishness. He called it "respect for women." He was married to one and father to three and never spoke about breasts or bottoms or private parts around his boys. Once I heard him say, "for every Jack, a Jill" as we watched an especially slovenly couple, suffering what are now called various "fashion disasters" or "wardrobe malfunctions" as they left a roadhouse under the evident influence of strong drink. They climbed on their motorcycle and sped headlong into traffic as the light we waited at had just turned green. "For every Jack a Jill," he said. Then, I suppose, wanting to moderate the criticism, lest he be a bad example to his son, he said, "God is good," and left it there.

Which brings me back around to what I meant to focus on, neither the rump muscles, nor sphincters, nor the humans who put us in mind of same, rather, *Equus asinus*— the sure-footed, horse-like, domesticated mammal we associate with the stubborn and steadfast, Bethlehem and Palm Sunday. And how this wee beast has become for me a sort of cipher for the brotherhood of man, the fraternity of fellow miscreants, a key by which I gain access to the wider kinship shared with everything.

> When fishes flew and forests walked
> And figs grew upon thorn,
> Some moment when the moon was blood
> Then surely I was born.
>
> With monstrous head and sickening cry
> And ears like errant wings,
> The devil's walking parody
> On all four-footed things.[1]

Thus does G. K. Chesterton, in his poem "The Donkey," profess the amalgam of man and beast at the core of the human condition.

When I look into the gob of my piebald jack, I see the faces of my fellow man—each of us the same but different. Townsmen and countrymen, strangers in the daily traffic, athletes at their triumphs and heartbreaks, politicos elected to higher office, members of the reverend clergy—are we not all asses, after all? Why else would I hear in my donkey's yawping the existential dread of Everyman, the Fellow Traveler, the brotherhood at large?

What—you are possibly asking yourself—is that jackass talking about?

Possibly I've gotten ahead of myself.

I keep a small home on the west coast of Ireland—a freehold I inherited from my late cousin, Nora, a spinster who went to her reward in her ninetieth year, early in the last decade of the last century. It is the house my great-grandfather left in 1890 to find his future in lower Michigan. He married a woman named Ryan, sired a teacher, a priest, and a civil servant—like winning the trifecta for the immigrant Irish—and died never seeing the homeplace again. Neither did any of his children, or grandchildren. Eight decades after his emigration, I was the first of his line to return, and two decades after that, Nora, my dear and distant cousin, was the last in her line to take her leave. To paraphrase Paul writing to Romans: all things work together for some good. She left the "house and haggards, out-offices and cow-cabins" to me and, at my suggestion, she left the adjacent acres of pasturage and meadow to P.J. Roche, the young farmer who, together with his wife Breda, were Nora's helpmates and caretakers in her later years. It's a long time now since P.J. and I, over pints in a pub in Carrigaholt, came to the first of our many agreements. He knew I'd be her heir and executor. "Take care of her," is what I told him, "and I'll take care of you."

This windswept, treeless townland of Moveen, on the westernmost peninsula of County Clare, the narrowing land between the River Shannon's mouth and the North Atlantic, got electric light in the 1950s, slate roofs in the 1960s, and the great civilizers—the four T's I call them: tractors, toilets, television, and telephones—at the rate of roughly one per decade after that until I found myself at the turn of the current millennium, the here-again and gone-tomorrow, twice or thrice a yearly occupant of my ancestral home, looking out the window the ancients in my family looked out of, on all that changes and that never does.

I got Charles in the spring of 2002, for two hundred euros. These were the days of the Celtic Tiger and the value of asses seemed self-evident. He was just gone two—a fledgling, untested, but full of promise. I named him for the prince on the neighboring island, a man of my own vintage and history, postwar, pampered, the son of a queen. It was the ears, the breedy look of self-importance, the soupcon of insult and homage in the namesaking. It's a character flaw, I confess aloud. I have not prayed sufficiently for its removal.

I let him into the overgrown cottage yard—the "haggard" as it is called in West Clare—an L-shaped field that bounds the house, bordered by stone walls and ditch banks, whitethorn and alders, fuchsia and olearia. There's some shelter from the worst of weather off the ocean just two fields away. It was the field where a sickly cow or newborn calf or pony foal might be kept for easy access by the vet or householder. It was the yard in which, in former times, before the first Ford tractor ever appeared, the ass and cart were kept that hauled milk to the creamery every day, or dung to the meadows every other season, or the faithful to their weekly liturgies.

Maybe this is why Charles took to it like coming home, when in fact he'd never stepped foot in it before. First he buckled the hinges of his legs, fell to the ground, rolled on his broad back, hooves in the air, and bathed in the earth and dirt of it all, like a pope kissing the tarmac upon landing in a new nation, to signal, I suppose, his regard for the place. In no time he went to work, gobbling up the greensward, shitting and pissing at intervals, sleeping under the hedgerows, staring at the wall. I could see in his routine, which I monitored closely from the kitchen windows, something like my own—an effort to achieve some healthy balance between contemplation and production, intake and output, ease and effort. His appetite for the mundane and quotidian seemed, like mine, insatiable—endlessly chewing on his surroundings, his attention always cast earthward or straight ahead, considering the intersection of two walls for hours, as if the blank corner he stared into held the key to the mysteries of the universe, much as I sometimes get myself cornered—so fixed and wriggling between the past and future that I'm blind to the here and now I occupy.

In time I took to standing out in the haggard with him, a kind of daily office, an hour every afternoon, between the morning's labor and the evening's, an exercise in reconnection with my place and time. I would clear my mind and consider only what was in the moment—the small birds at the berries in the whitethorn, the constant hiss and din of the sea over the high neighboring fields, the sweet aromas of slurry and silage, the rain or the drizzle or the lack of same. It hardly mattered. In time I began saying mindless things to Charles, who would consider me from a safe distance and make no effort at response and seemed in all ways incurious about my being. He would approach at an angle for a whiff of me and turn away just as I'd extend a hand to scratch the broad flat forehead between his huge brown eyes, which put me in mind—can I be forgiven this?—of my true love's eyes which are of the same deep, inextinguishable hue. The monk's life that I lead in Moveen—the townland in West Clare I call home—distant from the pleasures of the flesh are to blame, no doubt, for such imaginings.

His indifference to me had its advantages. I told him things I knew he'd never repeat: the depth of my contempt for certain people who oughtn't be named in a public document, my disappointments, in general and in particular, my hopes for the future, however outlandish. Nor did my low-grade, free-range, ever-present existential fears—a feature in men of a certain age—about life and time, the way of the world, the proper conduct of love with another of your species; none of that bothered him. I could speak them outright in the same voice as I might read the daily paper and he'd take it all quite literally in stride.

I gave him, truth be told, my "shilling life" borrowing Auden's trope, "all the facts."

None of these confessions seemed to shock or bother

him. Nor any of the little verbal barbs I'd test his attention with. "What an ass!" I would say with aimed ambivalence. Nothing in his comportment changed. Nothing would budge him from insuperable calm.

It was the next year or the next one that Charles began to bray with purpose. He was a full stallion now, come of age, all ache and desire. I knew his pain. My sighting, for the first time, of his massive erection, a thing which seemed, as in most male things, apart from him and yet himself, explained the roar he would wake me with most mornings. By now we'd become truly brethren—me seeing in him the perfect confessor and scape-ass, able to bear whatever burdens I brought him of rage or love or dread or their variations. I'd found that a bucket of rolled oats, soaked overnight in warm water, would make him endure my touching him. I'd hold the bucket in one hand while he bent to sup from it, and with the other I would pet him. The sound of his chewing was soothing to me. I thought it might be a balm to himself and divert him from the pains of his chastity. I'd scratch the broad flat of his noggin, under his jawbone, between his ears. I bought a stiff brush at the grocers and found he'd stand for my using it on his back and hindquarters. I loved brushing the tuft of dark hair that formed the cross on his back—a feature in his breed which bore, of old, the burdens of young, virgin girls and saviors. The closing quatrains of Chesterton's poem were by now committed to memory.

> The tattered outlaw of the earth,
> Of ancient crooked will;
> Starve, scourge, deride me: I am dumb,
> I keep my secret still.

> Fools! For I also had my hour;
> One far fierce hour and sweet:
> There was a shout about my ears,
> And palms before my feet.[2]

Was it the stoic Epictetus who said we are given two ears and one mouth for a reason? I listened intently to my donkey's braying and discerned in it a racket often coincident with some darker urges.

It took me until the summer of the following year to find a suitable consort for Charles. I'd kept an eye on the want ads and the little notices that appear in shop windows. I made discreet enquires at the marts and fairs. I went to Mullagh and Spancil Hill and the county show in search of a mare ass to quiet him. When I found the little piebald filly, just gone two, at Michael Morgan's tidy farm near Inagh, I knew she was the one for him. I plunked down the thousand euros he had the brass to ask for her, having made out I was a Yank when I called on the phone.

And when I saw them in the haggard together I knew that mighty nature would take care of itself and that Charles and Camilla, as I could not help but call her, those lovebirds having lately pledged their troth, would become the stuff of song and story.

Years have passed since then, of course. There is too much to account for—races and trophies, heartbreaks and triumphs, epics and offspring—too much to account here in the here and now. Except for the lessons I've learned by watching them, Charles and Camilla out in the yard, huddled together in all different weathers, the Celtic tiger gone, the prodigals returned, that history makes asses of us all.

Chapter Twelve

The Good Funeral
and the Empty Tomb

A man that I work with named Wesley Rice once spent all of one day and all night carefully piecing together the parts of a girl's cranium. She'd been murdered by a madman with a baseball bat after he'd abducted and raped her. The morning of the day it all happened she'd left for school dressed for picture day—a schoolgirl dressed to the nines, waving at her mother, ready for the photographer. The picture was never taken. She was abducted from the bus stop and found a day later in a stand of trees just off the road a township south of here. After he'd raped her and strangled her and stabbed her, he beat her head with a baseball bat, which was found beside the child's body. The details were reported dispassionately in the local media along with the speculations as to which of the wounds was the fatal one—the choking, the knife or the baseball bat. No doubt these speculations were the focus of the double postmortem the medical examiner performed on her body before signing the death certificate "Multiple Injuries." Most embalmers, faced with what Wesley Rice was faced with after he'd opened

the pouch from the morgue, would have simply
said "closed casket," treated the remains enough
to control the odor, zipped the pouch and gone
home for cocktails. It would have been easier. The
pay was the same. Instead, he started working.
Eighteen hours later the girl's mother, who had
pleaded to see her, saw her. She was dead, to be
sure, and damaged; but her face was hers again, not
the madman's version. The hair was hers, not his.
The body was hers, not his. Wesley Rice had not
raised her from the dead nor hidden the hard facts,
but he had retrieved her death from the one who
had killed her. He had closed her eyes, her mouth.
He'd washed her wounds, sutured her lacerations,
pieced her beaten skull together, stitched the inci-
sions from the autopsy, cleaned the dirt from under
her fingernails, scrubbed the fingerprint ink from
her fingertips, washed her hair, dressed her in jeans
and a blue turtleneck, and laid her in a casket beside
which her mother stood for two days and sobbed
as if something had been pulled from her by force.
It was the same when her pastor stood with her
and told her "God weeps with you." And the same
when they buried the body in the ground. It was
then and always will be awful, horrible, unappeas-
ably sad. But the outrage, the horror, the heartbreak
belonged, not to the murderer or to the media or to
the morgue, each of whom had staked their claims
to it. It belonged to the girl and to her mother.
Wesley had given them the body back. "Barbaric"
is what Jessica Mitford called this "fussing over the
dead body." I say the monster with the baseball bat
was barbaric. What Wesley Rice did was a kindness.
And, to the extent that it is easier to grieve the loss
that we see, than the one we imagine or read about
in papers or hear of on the evening news, it was
what we undertakers call a good funeral.

It served the living by caring for the dead.[1]

A good funeral? I first heard that oddly oxymoronic trope from my father, who would come home from the office, throw his black suit coat on the back of a kitchen chair, undo his tie and top button of his starched white shirt, and sit down to dinner saying, "we had a couple good funerals today." It made perfect sense when he said it, and in the saying was implied the sense that a funeral might just as easily go bad. But what exactly makes a funeral good?

> After these things, Joseph of Arimathea, who was a disciple of Jesus, though a secret one because of his fear of the Jews, asked Pilate to let him take away the body of Jesus. Pilate gave him permission; so he came and removed his body. Nicodemus, who had at first come to Jesus by night, also came, bringing a mixture of myrrh and aloes, weighing about a hundred pounds. They took the body of Jesus and wrapped it with the spices in linen cloths, according to the burial custom of the Jews. Now there was a garden in the place where he was crucified, and in the garden there was a new tomb in which no one had ever been laid. And so, because it was the Jewish day of Preparation, and the tomb was nearby, they laid Jesus there. (John 19:38–42)

Joseph of Arimathea became the de facto patron saint of undertakers because he knew that a good funeral got the living where they needed to go by getting the dead where they needed to be—before the Sabbath, before the feast, before the celebration of life, the dead need to be tended to.

I'm not, I should say, entirely untutored in the scriptural, canonical, and pseudepigraphal; in fact, we have hosted a Bible study in my funeral home for the past several years.

Thus do the verses surrounding the burial of Christ, "according to the burial custom of the Jews," take on a personal relevance, because they affirm that every tribe and sect, religious and ethnic community is obliged to figure out what to do with their dead. And so when Joseph the Arimathean, in league with Nicodemus, petitioned Pilate for the body of Christ, they were acting out a primal office of their species and the particular dictates of their tribe. Men and women of a certain age pay attention to such observances.

It was much the same that early April years ago at the Vatican, when long-suffering Pope John Paul II finally died.

That first week of April 2005 was dominated by images of the dead man's body vested in red, mitered and laid out among the faithful with bells and books and candles, blessed with water and incense, borne from one station to the next in what began to take shape as a final journey. The front pages above the fold of the world's daily papers were uniform in their iconography: a corpse clothed in sumptuous vestments from head to toe, still as stone and horizontal. Such images, flickering across their ubiquitous screens, no doubt gave pause to many Americans for whom the presence of the dead at their own funerals had gone, strangely, out of style.

For many bereaved North Americans, the "celebration of life" involves a guest list open to everyone except the actual corpse, which is often dismissed, disappeared without rubric or witness, buried or burned, out of sight, out of mind, by paid functionaries such as me. So the visible presence of the pope's body at the pope's funeral struck many as an oddity, a quaint relic of old customs. How "Catholic" some predictably said, or how "Italian," or "Polish" or "traditional"; how "lavish," "expensive," or "barbaric." Such things were said after the deaths of Princess Diana and Ronald Reagan. "When in Rome," the perpetually beleaguered cable TV commentators would say, et cetera, et cetera.

In point of fact, what happened in Rome that week a good few years ago now followed a pattern as old as the species—it was "human," this immediate focus on the dead and this sense that the living must go the distance with them. Most of nature does not stop for death. But we do. Wherever our spirits go, or don't, ours is a species that has learned to process grief by processing the objects of our grief, the bodies of the dead, from one place to the next. We bear mortality by bearing mortals—the living and the dead—to the brink of a uniquely changed reality: Heaven or Valhalla or Whatever Is Next. We commit and commend them into the nothingness or somethingness, into the presence of God or God's absence. Whatever afterlife there is or isn't, human beings have marked their ceasing to be by going the distance with their dead, getting them to the brink of a new reality—to the tomb or the fire or the grave, the holy tree or deep sea, whatever sacred space of oblivion we consign them to. And we've been doing this since the beginning.

Our theology is shaped by our eschatology; our living faith informed by our best hopes for the dead; our ideas of God informed by our contemplation of Last Things— dying, death, heaven and hell, the judgment with its punishments and rewards.

Thus, the defining truth of our Christianity—the empty tomb—proceeds from the defining truth of our humanity: we fill them. Our mortality is certain though our faith lays claim to more. The mystery of the resurrection to eternal life is bound inextricably to the certainty of the cross of suffering and death. Indeed, the effort to make sense of it all—the religious impulse—owes to our primeval questions about the nature of death. Save for these uniquely human curiosities about last things and eschatologies and the liturgies we construct to answer them, we would be so much roadkill and windfall, litter and landfill, our names and dates, our lives and deaths unmarked and unremarkable. Like baptisms and nuptials, we do funerals to address the uniquely human questions—what is permanent, what is passing, what is the meaning of life and love, suffering and death. Gladioli and goldfish are not much troubled by these things. Only humans are.

You can try this at home.

If you have a pair of parakeets or Pomeranians, geraniums or cacti—just about any animate being will do—put one to death or simply let it die in its own good time and watch what the other of its own kind does. There may be some sniffing or circling in momentary scrutiny but little else will happen. The surviving half of the former duo will simply swim or slink or saunter away, keeping whatever thoughts they have to themselves.

We humans are different and it was ever thus.

Ours is the species bound to the dirt, fashioned from it, according to the book of Genesis (Gen. 2:7). Thus human and humus occupy the same page of our dictionaries because we are beings "of the soil," of the earth. The lexicon and language are full of such wisdoms. Thus, our "humic densities," as the scholar Robert Pogue Harrison calls it: the notion that everything human—our architecture and history, our monuments and cities, all rooted in and rising from the humus, the earth, the ground in which our dead are buried—is what eventually defines us.

Years ago I took to trying to imagine the first human widow awakening to the dead lump of a fellow next to her, stone still under the hides that covered and warmed them against the elements. This might have been forty or fifty thousand years ago, somewhere in the Urals or Mesopotamia or the Dordogne. Or maybe Lebanon or Uganda or the Congo and seventy or eighty thousand years ago. The species' history is a work in progress. Anyway, this is long before we have alphabets or agriculture, or any of the later-day civilizers. The species evolves from upright foragers and carnivores to upright foragers and carnivores who begin to think in symbolic terms. They begin to wonder. Symbol and image and icon and metaphor become part of their reality. What was it, I ask myself, that first vexed them into contemplations.

I always imagine a cave and primitive tools and art and

artifacts. They have fire and some form of language and social orders. This first human widow wakes up to find the man she's been sleeping with and cooking for and breeding with gone cold and quiet in a way she had not formerly considered. Depending on the weather, sooner or later she begins to sense that something about him has changed quite utterly and irreversibly. Probably she smells the truth of this within a matter of a day or two. And what makes her human is that she figures she'd better do something about it.

Let us, for a moment, consider her options.

Perhaps she gathers her things together and follows the nomadic herd of her group elsewhere, leaving the cave to him, in which case we could call it his tomb. Or maybe she likes the decor of the place and has put some of herself into the improvements so decides that she should stay and that the now unresponsive and decomposing lump of matter next to her should be removed. She drags him out by the ankles and begins her search for a cliff to push him over or a ditch to push him into or maybe she digs a pit in the earth to bury him because she doesn't want wild animals attracted to his odor. Or maybe she builds a fire, a large fire, around and atop his rotting body and feeds it with fuel until the body is all but consumed. Maybe she keeps one of the bones for a totem or remembrance. Or let's say she lives near a body of water and counts on the fish to cleanse his remains; or maybe she hoists him into a tree and figures the birds will pick him clean. Maybe she enlists the assistance of others of her kind in the performance of these duties who do their part sensing that they may need exactly this kind of help in the future.

And here is where, in my imagination of this, Humanity 101 becomes the course of our history. It has to do with that momentary pause before she turns and leaves the cave, or the ditch or the pit or the fire or the pond or the tree or whatever oblivion she has chosen for him. In that pause she stares into the oblivion she has consigned him to and frames what are the signature questions of our species: *Is that all there is? Why is he cold? Can this happen to me? What comes next?* Of course, there are other questions, many more, but all of them are uniquely human, because no other species ponders such things. And they align with questions that might have formed the first time she had sex or the first time she gave birth or the first time she was frightened by something in the sky or the dark. This is when the first glimpse of a life before or beyond this one begins to flicker into the species' consciousness and questions about where we come from and where we go take up more and more of the moments not spent on rudimentary survival. Maybe the way the sun rises and sets or the seasons change or the tide ebbs and flows begin to replicate her own existence. And maybe whatever made the larger and the smaller lights in the night sky and great yellow disk that moves across the sky had something to do with her and the man whose body she is after disposing of.

And this is the point that I am trying to make: that the contemplation of the existential mysteries, those around being and ceasing to be, is what separates humans from the rest of creation; and that our humanity is, therefore, directly tied to how we respond to mortality. In short, how we deal with our dead in their physical reality and how we deal with death as an existential reality define and describe us in primary ways. Furthermore, the physical reality of death and the existential contemplation of the concept of death are inextricably linked so that it can be said, in trying to define what might be among the first principles of humanity, that *ours is the species that deals with death (the idea of the thing) by dealing with our dead (the physical fact of the thing itself)*.

Insofar as our *Homo sapiens neanderthalensis*—our first human widow all those millennia ago—is concerned, it was by dealing with the corpse of her dead man that she began to deal with the concept of death. This intimate connection between the mortal corpse and the concept of mortality, it goes without saying, is at the core of our religious, artistic, scientific, and social impulses.[2]

"No form of human life," writes the sociologist Zygmunt Bauman in *Mortality, Immortality and Other Life Strategies*, "has been found that failed to pattern the treatment of deceased bodies and their posthumous presence in the memory of the descendants. Indeed, the patterning has been found so universal that discovery of graves and cemeteries is generally accepted by the explorers of prehistory as the proof that a humanoid strain whose life was never observed directly had passed the threshold of humanhood."[3]

I want to emphasize that Bauman finds two elements to this "threshold of humanhood." First, "to pattern the treatment of deceased bodies," and secondly, "their [the dead's] presence in the memory of descendants." And when we find evidence of ancient graves and cemeteries, crematories or other sites of final disposition, we can assume that they are venues where humans sought to deal with death by dealing with their dead—by treating their deceased bodies in ways that said they intended to keep "their posthumous presence in [their] memory."

And this formula—dealing with death by dealing with the dead—defined and described and, by the way, worked for humans for forty or fifty thousand years all over the planet, across every culture until we come to the most recent generations of North Americans, who for the past forty or fifty years, have begun to avoid and outsource and ignore their obligations to deal with the dead. They are willing enough to keep "their presence in the memory of descendants" (the idea of the thing), so long as they don't have to deal with "the treatment of deceased bodies" (the thing itself). A picture on the piano is fine, but public wakes, bearing the dead to open graves or retorts, is strictly out of fashion.

The bodiless obsequy, which has become a staple of available options for bereaved families in the past half century, has created an estrangement between the living and the dead that is unique in human history. Furthermore, this estrangement, this disconnect, this refusal to deal with our dead (their corpses), could be reasonably expected to handicap our ability to deal with death (the concept, the idea of it).

And a failure to deal authentically with death may have something to do with an inability to deal authentically with life.

It bears mentioning that while this estrangement is coincident with the increased use of cremation as a method of disposing of the dead over the same half century, and may be correlated to it, cremation is not the cause of this estrangement. Indeed, cremation is an ancient and honorable and effective method of body disposition, but in most cultures where it is practiced it is done publicly in ceremonial and commemorative venues, whereas in North America very often it is consigned to an off-site, out-of-sight, industrial venue where everything is handled privately and efficiently. Only in North America has cremation lost its ancient connection to fire, because it is so rarely actually witnessed. In North America, in the past fifty years, cremation has become synonymous with disappearance, not so much an alternative to burial or entombment, but rather an alternative to having to bother with the dead body.

Ours is a species that deals with death (the idea, the concept, the human condition) by dealing with the dead (the thing itself, in the flesh, the corpse). Whatever our responses to death might be—intellectual, philosophical, religious, ritual, social, emotional, cultural, artistic, et cetera—they are firstly and undeniably connected to the embodied remnant of the person who was. And while the dead can be pictured and imagined and conjured by symbol and metaphor, photo and recording, our allegiance and our primary obligations ought to be to the real rather than the virtual dead. In as much as a death in the family is primarily occasioned by the presence of a corpse, the emergent, immediate, collective, and purposeful response to that emergency is what a funeral is. In short, a funeral responds to the signature human concern, to wit, what to do about a dead human?

Thus, the presence of the dead is an essential, definitive element of a funeral. Funerals differ from all other commemorative events in that the presence of the dead and their subsequent disposition are primary concerns. Memorial services, celebrations of life, or variations on these commemorative events, whether held sooner or later or at intervals or anniversaries, in a variety of locales, while useful socially for commemorating the dead and paying tribute to their memories, lack an essential manifest and function, to wit, the disposition of the dead. In this sense, the option to dispose of the dead privately, through the agency of hirelings, however professional they might be, and however moving the memorial that follows may be, is an abdication of an essential undertaking and fundamental humanity.

A second essential, definitive element of a funeral is that there must be those to whom the death matters. A death happens to both the one who dies and to those who survive the death and are affected by it. If no one cares, if there is no one to mark the change that has happened, if there is no one to name and claim the loss and the memory of the dead, then the dead assume the status of Bishop Berkeley's tree falling noiselessly in the forest: if no one hears it, it did not fall, it never was. It is the same with humans. And like Bishop Berkeley, it may become for us the case for a God who sees and hears and claims everything in creation.

A third essential, definitive element of a funeral is that there must be some narrative, some effort toward an answer, however provisional, of those signature human questions about what death means for both the one who has died and those to whom it matters. Thus, an effort to broker some peace between the corpse and the mourners by describing the changed reality death occasions is part of the essential response to mortality. Very often this is a religious narrative.

Often it is written in a book, the text of which is widely read. Or it might be philosophical, artistic, intellectual—a poem in place of a psalm, a song in place of prayer—either way there must be some case to be made for what has happened to the dead and what the living might expect because of it. "Behold, I show you a mystery," or words to that effect are often heard.

A fourth and final essential, definitive element of a funeral is that it must accomplish the disposition of the dead. They are not welcome, we know intuitively, to remain among us in the way they were while living. Furthermore, it is by getting the dead where they need to go that the living get where they need to be. And while this disposition often involves the larger muscles and real work, it also enacts our essential narratives, assists in the process of our essential emotions, images, and intellection about the dead, and fixes their changed status in the landscape of our future and daily lives, whether the dead are buried, burned, entombed, enshrined, or scattered, hoist into the air, cast into the sea, or left out for the scavenging birds, our choice of their oblivion makes their disposition palatable, acceptable, maybe even holy, and our participation in it remedial, honorable, maybe even holy.

These four essential, definitive elements, then: the corpse, the caring survivors, some brokered change of status between them, and the disposition of the dead make a human funeral what it is.

Finally, once we can separate the essential elements from the accessories, the fundamental obligations from fashionable options, the substance from the stuff, the necessary from the knickknacks, the core from the pulp, we might be able to assign relative measures of worth to what we do when one of our own kind dies. We might be able to figure not only the costs but the values. Thus, coffin and casket, mum plants and carnations, candles and pall, vaults and monuments, limousines and video tributes—all of them accessories, nonessentials. They may be a comfort but they are nonessential. Same for funeral directors and rabbis, sextons and pastors, priests and clerks, florists and lawyers and hearse drivers—all of them accessories who may, nonetheless, assist the essential purpose of a funeral. And when we do; when we endeavor to serve the living by caring for the dead, we are assisting in the essential, definitive work of the funeral and the species that devised this deeply and uniquely human response to death.

So much of what I know of final things I have learned from the reverend clergy: these men and women of God who drop what they're doing and come on the run when there is trouble. These are the local heroes who show up, armed only with faith, who respond to calls in the middle of the night, the middle of dinner, the middle of already busy days to bedsides and roadsides, intensive care and emergency rooms, nursing homes and hospice wards and family homes, to try and make some sense of senseless things. They are on the front lines, holy corpsmen in the flesh-and-blood combat between hope and fear. Their faith is contagious and emboldening. Their presence is balm and anointing. The Lutheran pastor who always sang the common doxology at graveside, "Praise God from Whom All Blessings Flow," his hymn sung into the open maw of unspeakable sadness, startling in its comfort and assurance. The priest who would intone the Gregorian chant and tribal Latin of the In Paradisum while leading the pallbearers to the grave, counting on the raised voice and ancient language to invoke the heavenly and earthly hosts. The young Baptist preacher who, at a loss for words, pulled out his harmonica and played the mournful and familiar notes of "Just As I Am" over the coffin of one of our town's most famous sinners. "Between the stirrup and the ground," he quietly promised the heartsore family and upbraided the too eagerly righteous, "mercy sought and mercy found."

My friend Jake Andrews, an Episcopal priest, now dead

for years but still remembered, apart from serving his little local parish was chaplain to the fire and police departments and became the default minister, the go-to guy for the churchless and lapsed among our local citizenry. Father Andrews always rode in the hearse with me, whether the graveyard was minutes or hours away, in clement and inclement weather, and whether there were hundreds or dozens or only the two of us to hear, he would stand and read the Holy Script such as it had been given him to do. When cremation became, as it did, the norm among his townspeople and congregants, he would leave the living to the tea and cakes and ices in the parish hall and ride with me and the dead to the crematory. There he would perform his priestly offices with the sure faith and deep humanity that seems to me an imitation of Christ. It was Jake Andrews's belief that pastoral care included care of the saints he was called on to bury and cremate. Baptisms and weddings were, he said, "easy duties," whereas funerals were "the deep end of the pool." I think he had, as we all do, his dark nights of the soul, his wrestling with angels, his reasonable doubts. His favorite studies were on the book of Job. But still, he believed the dead to be alive in Christ. He met the mourners at the door and pressed the heavens with their lamentations. It was Jake who taught me the power of presence, the work of mercy in the showing up, pitching in, bearing our share of whatever burden, and going the distance with the living and the dead. He taught me that a living faith ought not be estranged from death's rudiments and duties. Faith claims based upon redemptive suffering and meaningful death, a risen corpse and an empty tomb, lose something of their power when the living become so distant and estranged from the shoulder work and shovel work the dead require.

The question presents itself: what harm if we simply forget how to do a good funeral? What harm if we grow more distant from our dead?

Or ought we ask, as more and more of our fellow Americans are joining the church of "none of the above" when it comes to religious identity, is there any connection between the slow but steady decline in church attendance, community and identity, and the pop culture's seemingly insatiable interest in "True Blood," and "Twilight" and "The Walking Dead" and the kindred popularity of Zombie Apocalypse? Are the erotically charged vamps and vampires served up by Hollywood somehow connected to the failure of our "eschatological nerve," as Dr. Thomas Long elegantly calls the slow but steady erosion of relevance of the Christian message in its current telling?[4]

These are queries beyond my scope or scholarship; still, it seems to me a simple thing, that we should restore to the funeral some aspect of goodness, some gravity and tasking, some actual purpose, some shoulder and shovel work, some witness at the very least.

It has taken all of fifty-five years, from the year that Jessica Mitford published her lampoon of funeral practices, *The American Way of Death*, the same year we buried President John F. Kennedy, to downsize and devolve the funeral from an exercise in eschatology to a celebration of biography. No longer do we process mortality by processing mortals from the spaces they inhabited in life to the stations they inhabit after death. No longer do we accompany them with singing. We hardly accompany them at all. No longer the lapsed Catholic or backslidden Baptist, devout Calvinist, holy roller or born again. Now we are bowlers and bikers and golfers and gardeners. We are known less for what we believed and more for how we passed our time. Rather than affirm a salvation of faith and baptism and religious practice, we "celebrate" the life of barbecues and hobbies in a kind of funeral karaoke in which the good laugh is approved and the good cry is discouraged.

As baby boomers age and watch the sacred faith-claims of the church replaced by funerals-lite, the happy-chat silliness of "open mic" eulogies typical of bodiless obsequies and memorial services, it is little wonder that we see more and more formerly observant Christians join the ranks of the "spiritual but not religious." As the dead are disappeared from their funerals, and heaven and hell have become virtual and vaporous, the faith claims we remember from our youth become more and more vacuous. We neither see the dead nor believe anymore in the sacred mysteries of their redemption or salvation.

Perhaps if the dead are more welcomed in church, the full heft and flesh of their corpses afforded their sacred space at the foot of the altar and in holy ground, their burden carried from station to station by the large muscles of real grief and faith, maybe then the living will find more reasons to return.

Chapter Thirteen

The Sin-eater

Argyle the sin-eater came the day after—
a narrow, hungry man whose laughter
and the wicked upturn of his one eyebrow
put the local folks in mind of trouble.
But still they sent for him and sat him down
amid their whispering contempts to make
his table near the dead man's middle,
and brought him soda bread and bowls of beer
and candles, which he lit against the reek
that rose off that impenitent cadaver
though bound in skins and soaked in rosewater.
Argyle eased the warm loaf right and left
and downed swift gulps of beer and venial sin
then lit into the bread now leavened with
the corpse's cardinal mischiefs, then he said
"Six pence, I'm sorry." And the widow paid him.
Argyle took his leave then, down the land
between hay-ricks and Friesians with their calves
considering the innocence in all
God's manifold creation but for Man,
and how he'd perish but for sin and mourning.

Two parishes between here and the ocean:
a bellyful tonight is what he thought,
please God, and breakfast in the morning.[1]

A rgyle, the sin-eater, came into being in the hard winter
of 1984. My sons were watching a swashbuckler
on TV—*The Master of Ballantrae*—based on Robert Louis
Stevenson's novel about Scots brothers and their imbroglios. I was dozing in the wingback after a long day at the
funeral home, waking at intervals too spaced to follow the
narrative arc.

But one scene I half wakened to—the gauzy edges of
memory still give way—involved a corpse laid out on a board
in front of a stone tower house, kinsmen and neighbors
gathered round in the grey, sodden moment. Whereupon
a figure of plain force, part pirate, part panhandler, dressed
in tatters, unshaven and wild-eyed, assumed what seemed a
liturgical stance over the body, swilled beer from a wooden
bowl and tore at a heel of bread with his teeth. Wiping his
face on one arm, with the other he thrust his open palm at
the woman nearest him. She pressed a coin into it spitefully
and he took his leave. Everything was grey: the rain and fog,
the stone tower, the mourners, the corpse, the countervailing ambivalences between the widow and the horrid man.
Swithering is the Scots word for it—to be of two minds,
in two realities at once: grudging and grateful, faithful and
doubtful, broken and beatified—caught between a mirage
and an apocalypse. The theater of it was breathtaking, the
bolt of drama. I was fully awake. It was over in ten, maybe
fifteen seconds.

I knew him at once.

The scene triggered a memory of a paragraph I'd read
twelve years before in mortuary school, from *The History of
American Funeral Directing*, by Robert Habenstein and William Lamers. I have that first edition, by Bulfin Printers of
Milwaukee circa 1955.

The paragraph in chapter 3, page 128 at the bottom reads:

A nod should be given to customs that disappeared. Puckle tells of a curious functionary, a sort of male scapegoat called the "sin-eater." It was believed in some places that by eating a loaf of bread and drinking a bowl of beer over a corpse, and by accepting a six-pence, a man was able to take unto himself the sins of the deceased, whose ghost thereafter would no longer wander.[2]

The "Puckle" referenced was Bertram S. Puckle, a British scholar, whose *Funeral Customs: Their Origin and Development* would take me another forty years to find and read. But the bit of cinema and the bit of a book had aligned like tumblers of a combination lock clicking into place and opening a vault of language and imagination.

I was raised by Irish Catholics. Even as I write that it sounds a little like "wolves" or some especially feral class of creature. Not in the apish, nativist sense of immigrant hordes, rather in the fierce faith and family loyalties, the pack dynamics of their clannishness, their vigilance and pride. My parents were grandchildren of immigrants who had all married within their tribe. They'd sailed from nineteenth-century poverty into the prospects of North America, from West Clare and Tipperary, Sligo and Kilkenny, to Montreal and Ontario, upper and lower Michigan. Graces and O'Haras, Ryans and Lynches—they brought their version of the "one true faith," druidic and priest-ridden, punctilious and full of superstitions, from the boggy parishes of their ancients to the fertile expanse of middle America. These were people who saw statues move, truths about the weather in the way a cat warmed to the fire, omens about coming contentions in a pair of shoes left up on a table, bad luck in some numbers, good fortune in others. Odd lights in the nightscape foreshadowed death; dogs' eyes attracted lightning; the curse of an old woman could lay one low. The clergy were to be "given what's going to them," but otherwise, "not to be tampered with." Priests were feared and their favor curried—their curses and their blessings opposing poles of the powerful medicine they were known to possess. Everything had meaning beyond the obvious. The dead were everywhere and their ghosts inhabited the air and memory and their old haunts, real as ever, if in an only slightly former tense, in constant need of care and appeasement. They were, like the saints they'd been named for, prayed over, prayed to, invoked as protection against all enemies, their names recycled through generations, reassigned to new incarnations.

I was named for a dead priest, my father's uncle. Some few years after surviving the Spanish flu epidemic of 1918, he got "the call." ("Vocations follow famine," an old bromide holds. No less the flu?) He went to seminary in Detroit and Denver and was ordained in the middle of the Great Depression. We have a photo of his "First Solemn High Mass" on June 10, 1934, at St. John's Church in Jackson, Michigan, a block from the clapboard house he'd grown up in.

His father, my great-grandfather, another Thomas Lynch, did not live to get into this photo of women in print dresses and men in straw boaters on a sunny June Sunday between world wars. He had come from the poor townland of Moveen on the West Clare peninsula that forms the upper lip of the gaping mouth of the River Shannon—a treeless sloping plain between the ocean and the estuary, its plots of pasturage divided by hedgerows and intermarriages. He'd come to Michigan for the work available at the huge penitentiary there in Jackson where he painted cellblocks, worked in the laundry, and finished his career as a uniformed guard. He married a Ryan woman, fathered a daughter who taught, a son who got good work with the post office, and now a priest—like hitting the trifecta for a poor Irish "yank," all cushy jobs with reliable pensions. He never saw Ireland again.

In the middle of the retinue of family and parishioners, posed for the photo at the doors to the church around their freshly minted, homegrown priest, is my father, aged ten years, seated next to his father and mother, bored but obedient in his new knee breeches. Because the young priest— just going thirty—is sickly but willing, the bishop in Detroit will send him back out West to the bishop in Santa Fe who assigns him to the parish of Our Lady of Guadalupe, in Taos, in hopes that the high, dry air of the Sangre de Cristo Mountains might ease his upper respiratory ailments and lengthen his days.

He is going to die just two years later, of pneumonia, at the end of July 1936. The Apache women whose babies he baptized, whose sons he taught to play baseball, whose husbands he preached to, will process his rough-sawn coffin down the mountains from Taos, along the upper reaches of the Rio Grande, through landscapes Georgia O'Keeffe will make famous, to the cathedral in Santa Fe where Archbishop Rudolph Gerken will preside over his requiems, then send his body back to his people, COD, on a train bound for Michigan and other points east.

A moment that will shape our family destiny for generations occurs a couple days later in the Desnoyer Funeral Home in Jackson. The dead priest's brother, my grandfather, is meeting with the undertaker to sort details for the hometown funeral at St. John's. He brings along my father, now gone twelve, for reasons we can never know. While the two men are discussing plots and boxes, pallbearers and honoraria, the boy wanders through the old mortuary until he comes to the doorway of a room where he espies two men in shirtsleeves dressing a corpse in liturgical vestments. He stands and watches quietly. Then they carefully lift the freshly vested body of his dead uncle from the white porcelain table into a coffin. Then turn to see the boy at the door. Ever after my father will describe this moment—this elevation, this slow, almost ritual hefting of the body—as the one to which he will always trace his intention to become a funeral director. Might it have aligned in his imagination with that moment during the masses he attended at St. Francis de Sales when the priest would elevate the host and chalice, the putative body and blood of Christ, when bells were rung, heads bowed, breasts beaten in awe? Might he have conflated the corruptible and the incorruptible? The mortal and immortality? The sacred and the profane?

"Why," we would often ask him, "why didn't you decide to become a priest?"

"Well," he would tell us, matter-of-factly, "the priest was dead."

It was also true that he'd met Rosemary O'Hara that year, a redheaded fifth-grader who would become the girl of his dreams and who would write him daily when he went off to war with the Marines in the South Pacific; who would marry him when he came home and mother their nine children and beside whom he'd be buried half a century later.

"God works in strange ways," my mother would tell us, smiling wisely, passing the spuds, all of us marveling at the ways of things.

And so these "callings," such as they were, these summons to her life as a wife and mother and his to fatherhood and undertaking—a life's work he would always describe as "serving the living by caring for the dead" or a "corporal work of mercy"—and his sons and daughters and their sons and daughters who operate now half a dozen funeral homes in towns all over lower Michigan, all tied to that first week of August, 1936, and a boy watching two mortuary sorts lift the body of a dead priest into a box.

That was another received truth of his nunnish upbringing and our own—that life and time were not random accretions of happenstance. On the contrary, there was a plan for each and every one of us, and ours was only to discern our "vocation," our "calling," our purpose here. No doubt this is how the life of faith, the search for meaning, the wonder about the way of things first sidles up to the curious mind.

When I was seven, my mother sent me off to see the priest, to learn enough of the magic Latin—the language of ritual and mystery—to become an altar boy. Fr. Kenny, our parish priest at St. Columban's, was a native of Galway, had been at seminary with my father's uncle, and had hatched a plan with my sainted mother to guide me toward the holy orders. This, the two of them no doubt reckoned, was in keeping with the will of God—that I should fulfill the vocation and finish the work of the croupy and tubercular young man I'd been named for. I looked passably hallowed in cassock and surplice, I had a knack for the vowel-rich acoustics of Latin and had already intuited the accountancy of sin and guilt and shame and punishment so central to the religious life. This tuition I owed to *Father Maguire's Baltimore Catechism* and the Sister Servants of the Immaculate Heart of Mary who had prepared me for the grade school sacraments of confession and the Eucharist. I had learned to fast before Communion, to confess and do penance in preparation for the feast, to keep track of my sins by sort and number, to purge them by prayer and mortification, supplication and petition. To repair the damage done by impure thoughts or cursing at a sibling, a penance of Our Fathers and Hail Marys would be assigned. *Mea culpa, mea culpa, mea maxima culpa* became for me the breast-thumping idioms of forgiveness and food, purification and communion, atonement and satiety, reconciliation and recompense, which are so central to the "holy sacrifice of the Mass" we Catholic school kids daily attended. Thus were the connections between hunger and holiness, blight and blessedness, contrition and redemption, early on established, and these powerful religious metaphors gathered themselves around the common table. That sacred theater replayed itself each night at our family meals where our father and our blessed mother would enact a home version of the sacrifice and feast, the brothers and sisters and I returning prodigals for whom the fatted calf, incarnate as stew or goulash, burgers or casseroles, had been prepared.

On Fridays my father brought home bags of fish and chips. Whatever our sins were, they were forgiven.

"Introibo ad altare Dei" is what James Joyce had "stately, plump Buck Mulligan" intone, while holding a bowl of lather aloft, on the opening page of his epic *Ulysses*. Years later, reading that book for the first time, *Ad deum qui laetificat juventutem meam* still formed in my memory as the cadenced response to the gods who'd given joy to my youth. Irreverence seemed a proper seasoning by then, the grain of salt added to articles of faith.

For all of my mother's and the priest's well-intentioned connivances, and though I kept my ears peeled for it, I never ever heard the voice of God. I remember seeing the dead priest's cassock hanging from a rafter in my grandparents' basement, a box with his biretta and other priestly things on a shelf beside it. I tried them on but nothing seemed to fit. Over time my life of faith came to include an ambivalence about the church that ranged from passion to indifference—a kind of swithering, brought on, no doubt, by mighty nature—the certain sense awakened in me when I was twelve or thereabouts that among the good Lord's greatest gifts to humankind were the gifts he gave us of each other. Possibly it was meditating on the changes I could see in bodies all around me and sense in my own body, late in my grade-school years, that there were aspects of the priestly life that would be, thanks be to God, impossible for me.

I record these things because they seem somehow the ground and compost out of which Argyle rose, in that flash of recognition years ago, to become the mouthpiece for my mixed religious feelings. If I'd learned sin and guilt and shame and contrition from the nuns and priests, I was likewise schooled in approval and tolerance and inextinguishable love by my parents, earthen vessels though they were. Grace—the unmerited favor of Whoever is in Charge Here—was the gift outright of my upbringing. It made me—like the apostle that the priest I'd been named for was named for, a doubter and contrarian—grateful for religious sensibilities but wary of all magisterium.

By the end of winter that year I'd written three or four Argyle poems. I field-tested them at Joe's Star Lounge on North Main Street in Ann Arbor where boozers and poets would gather on Sunday afternoons to read their latest to one another. It was a kind of communion, I suppose, or potluck anyway: everyone bringing a "dish" to pass, their best home recipes of words. I liked the sound of them in my mouth, the cadence of Argyle's odd adventures and little blasphemies.

His name came easy—after the socks, of course, the only thing I knew that was reliably Scots, apart from whisky, and after the acoustic resemblance to "our guile," which sounded a note not far from "guilt," both notions that attached themselves to his invention.

These were the days long before one could Google up facts on demand, when writers were expected to just make things up out of the whole cloth of imagination: his loneliness, the contempt of locals, the contretemps of clergy. I intuited these, along with the sense of his rootlessness, his orphanage and pilgrimage. I'd spent, by then, enough time in the rural western parishes of Ireland and Scotland to have a sense of the landscapes and people he would find himself among—their "ground sense" and land passions, their religious sensibilities. And the two dozen lines of the first of these poems, each of the lines ranging between nine and a dozen syllables and thus conforming to an imprecise pentameter, seemed perfectly suited to the brief meditations and reliance on numbers and counts that were part of the churchy rubrics: stations of the cross, deadly sins, glorious and sorrowful mysteries, corporal and spiritual works of mercy, the book of hours. Hence this breviary: a couple dozen poems, a couple dozen lines each, a couple dozen photos, about which more anon.

By turns, of course, I began to identify with Argyle. As

the only funeral director in this small town in Michigan, I was aware of the ambivalence of human sorts toward anyone who takes on undertakings involving money and corpses, religious practice and residual guilt. Both undertaker and sin-eater know that people in need are glad to see you coming and gladder still to see you gone. Argyle fit my purposes and circumstances. The work to which he had, by force of hunger, been called, seemed in concert with my own summons and stumblings both religiously and occupationally. He is trying to keep body and soul together. And these poems articulate the mixed blessing and contrariety of my own life of faith—pre-Vatican II to the Current Disaster. I have been variously devout and devoutly lapsed.

The church of my childhood—the "holy mother" it called itself—has left no few of its children more damaged than doted over, more ignored than nurtured, orphaned and hungry, fed a thin gruel of religiosity rather than the loaves and fishes of spiritual sustenance. The ongoing failure of its management class, its up-line politics and old-boy malfeasances, have done remarkable damage to generations of faithful servant priests and faithful people.

Of course, the life of faith is never settled, driven as it must be by doubts and wonder, by those experiences, losses and griefs, that cast us adrift, set us to wander the deserts, wrestle with angels. And for Argyle, as for all fellow pilgrims, the tensions between community and marginalization, orthodoxy and apostasy, authority and autonomy, belonging and disbelief, keep him forever second-guessing where he stands with God. In this state of flux we are not alone.

The sin-eater is both appalled by his culture's religiosity and beholden to it. The accountancy of sin and punishment at once offends him and feeds him. He is caught in the struggle between views of damnation and salvation and the God he imagines as the loving parents he never knew—pure forgiveness, constant understanding, permanent love. He lives in constant hope and fear, despair and faith, gratitude and God hunger. In the end, he isn't certain but believes that everything is forgiven, whomever God is or isn't, everything is reconciled.

If the English master Auden was correct, and "art is what we do to break bread with the dead," then the Irish master Heaney was likewise correct when he suggests that "rhyme and meter are the table manners." Prayer and poetry are both forms of "raised speech" by which we attempt to commune with our makers and creation, with the gone but not forgotten. Argyle's hunger, his breaking bread upon the dead, is a metaphor for all those rituals and rubrics by which our kind seek to commune with those by whom we are haunted—the ghosts of those gone before us, parents and lovers, mentors and heroes, friends and fellow outcasts—who share with us this sweet humanity, our little moments, the sense we are always trying to make of it in words. His is a sacrament of renewal and restoration. It is in such communion that our hope is nourished—the hope that is signature to our species—that there may be something in nature's harmonium and hush discernable as the voice of God.

Much the same with icon and image—the things we see in which we might see other things, the hand of God or the hand of man partaking in the same creation. Thus these photographs, taken by my son, Michael, in his many visits to our home in Ireland—the house his great-great-grandfather came out of; the house to which I was the first of our family to return, now more than forty years ago; the house my great-great-grandfather was given as a wedding gift in the decade after the worst of the famines in the middle of the nineteenth century.

When I first went to Ireland—a young man with a high number in the Nixon draft lotto and, therefore, a future stretched out before me—I thought I'd see the forty shades of green. And though I arrived in the off-season, with a one-way ticket, no money or prospects, in a poor county of a poor country, as disappointing a Yank as ever there was,

I was welcomed by cousins who could connect me to the photo that hung on their wall of their cousin, a priest, who had died years before. They took me in, put me by the fire, fed me and gave me to believe that I belonged there, I was home. If there is a heaven it might feel like that. In the fullness of time, they left the house to me: a gift, a grace. Everything in those times seemed so black-and-white—the cattle, the clergy, the stars and dark, right and wrong, love and hate, the edges and borders all well-defined. But now it all seems like shades of grey, shadow and apparition, glimpses only, through the half-light of daybreak and gloaming, mirage and apocalypse, a kind of swithering. And so these photos of home fires and icons, landscapes and interiors, graveyards and coast roads, asses and cattle, statues and stone haunts— all in black-and-white and shades of grey: like doubt and faith, what may or mayn't be, what is or isn't, happenstance or the hand of God.

In the end, Argyle is just trying to find his way home, burdened by mighty nature, life's work and tuitions, he's looking for a place at a table where he is always welcome and never alone. In the end he is possessed of few certainties or absolutes, his faith always seasoned by wonder and doubt. He knows if there's a God, it is not him. If there is one, then surely we are all God's children, or none of us are. Either way, the greatest gifts are one another, the greatest sins against each other. To be forgiven, he must forgive everything, because God loves all children or none of them, forgives everything or forgives nothing at all, hears all our prayers or none of them.

At the end, all of his prayers have been reduced to thanks. All of the answers have become you're welcome.

Chapter Fourteen

Lacrimae Rerum: A Play in One Act

(In memory of John Callaghan, chorister, organist, father of a nation)

CHARACTERS IN THE PLAY

E. J. O'Curry—*A bachelor farmer in West Clare*
Sean Curtin—*A frequent visitor from America*
Fr. Michael Callaghan—*A parish priest*
Lourda Kearney—*A widowed publican*
The cremated remains of Margaret Mary O'Hara—*In an angel-shaped urn*

SETTING

The West Clare Peninsula of Ireland, between the North Atlantic and the River Shannon Estuary. It is the first of April, and Thursday in Holy Week, in the first year of the second decade of the new millennium.

SCENE 1

The kitchen of a small cottage in West Clare on the narrow peninsula between the ocean and estuary. The walls are white-washed plaster, the window small. There's a GAA calendar, a photo of the pope, a picture of the Sacred Heart with a small red electric cross in front of it. A rosary hangs from the corner of the picture. The deep window ledge is littered with newspapers and books. A table sits in the middle of the upstage wall, under the small window, with the tableware required for a single man. There is a red plastic washbasin, cups and saucers, plates and silverware. Three chairs—one ancient and overstuffed, and two sugan chairs, a little the worse for wear, sit stage right, assembled round an open hearth with soot stains on the wall at stage right. Opposite the fireplace, a large press holds a small TV, a radio, some family photos and oddments. There is a door to another room beside it.

Though early in the twenty-first century, the interior of the cottage suggests an earlier, simpler time. The floor is flagstone, the ceiling is vaulted. There is one bare light bulb hanging in the middle. There is no running water. A blue plastic bucket with water sits on a box by the door in the corner of the stage left.

E. J. O'Curry, bachelor and "chastitute," enters the kitchen from the bedroom door beside the fireplace, upstage right. He is a small farmer in his mid-seventies. He goes out the main door (upstage left) and after some moments returns, tucking his shirt in, zipping his fly, hitching his belt, and moves slowly about the kitchen, setting the kettle to boil, kindling a fire with paper and turf, grunting and groaning with the aches and pains of age and his hangover. He mumbles a little to himself, "You'll make water before you cross water, said Mrs. Morrissey years ago," bits of speeches and poems, "when you are old and grey and full of sleep," lines from old tunes, "the hare and the rabbit are plane to be seen." He is accustomed to being his own best company. He pulls the butt of a cigarette from his coat pocket, rummages through the litter of newspapers in the window ledge, finds a match, lights the cigarette, tosses the match into the fire and sits down in the overstuffed chair smoking and coughing, reading a scrap of newspaper in the late morning. The wind is up and howling. It is a spring morning, Holy Thursday.

A face appears briefly outside the small window. A familiar voice calls to him from out of doors.

SEAN: God bless all here!

E. J.: (*Startled by the early visit, rising from the chair to open the door.*) The living and the dead!

SEAN: And those with a boot in either side! Are you right there, E. J.? Am I waking you?

E. J.: Not yet, thanks be to God. Only moving slowly this morning, damaged by my habits and lapses.

He throws open the door. Cats run in from the outside, and Sean, standing in the doorway, enters the house carrying a canvas sack with two looped handles on it and a square box inside of it.

SEAN: Our own worst enemies.

E. J.: Isn't it just so, Sean. You're welcome to this part of the country!

SEAN: Am I waking you E. J.? I could come back later . . .

E. J.: Not at all! I'm up with hours. I broke out a little last night, and would you believe it, after three months without a drop. Come inside you'll be perished. Sit in there by the fire. Cripes but the weather is very broken. I wondered if you'd be back for the Easter. When did you come?

SEAN: (*Sitting in one of the sugan chairs, he places the canvas bag on the other, in the corner next to him. He warms his hands to the fire.*) Am after landing in Shannon this morning, then rented the car, then out here like a shot. Anything strange in the townland since?

E. J.: Not one solitary thing. (*The kettle whistles, E. J. rises to make the tea.*) We're all just doting away. Keeping body and soul together, not much more. When were you home last, Sean? Was it August? That's right, the donkey derby.

SEAN: Yes, August last year.

E. J.: I suppose Paddy Mac got married since then. A Carmody woman, from Sligo. It was September at the Armada, and a great night it was. And John

O'Donaghue, you heard about poor John. It's a cruel thing, so very sudden.

SEAN: The poor cratur. That was very sad.

E. J.: And how long have ye?

SEAN: I'll knock the month out of it, E. J., maybe more. My daughter's expecting the first of June and I'll have to be back in plenty of time for that. Wouldn't do to miss the blessed event, the nativity. Mary will give me the month but she'd hunt me after that.

E. J.: Fair play to her. How old is she now? Is she 30?

E. J. pours two cups, drops a little milk into both and a little sugar, gives a cup to his houseguest. Butters two pieces of soda bread. Gives one to Sean.

SEAN: Eat that yourself, E. J. I'm after the fry at the Old Ground. Mary? All right if she isn't nearly gone the sixty! But never say that I said so. That's nice tea, E. J. Couldn't beat the Green Label.

E. J.: No, Peg. How old is Peg?

SEAN: Gone 35. You don't feel the time going. And I do believe it's dicey enough business, for a woman of her age, the pregnancy, . . .

E. J.: No bother, I've a cow behind, fat with her fourteenth calf. She'll find her way into the haggard one of these evenings and calf away for herself. Same as your sweet Peg. No bother. Mighty nature.

SEAN: Mighty fecking nature indeed. Now you've said it E. J. And all of us yoked to it, like gravity—between oblivions—the womb and tomb, the gravid and the grave. Coming and going it's all the same: what's that your man said? "Sans teeth, sans hair, sans everything." Same drooling, piddling, incontinent mess. Just a different diaper, different nappies I suppose you call them here.

E. J.: Never mind your sans everything. Did you hear about the priest who asked the doctor for Viagree?

SEAN: Viagra?

E. J.: Viagra. An old P.P. goes to the doctor for a bottle of Viagra and tells your man to cut them up, first in halves and then in quarters and your man doesn't know what at all to make of it, but figures the priest must be told, all the same. "In point of fact, Father," says he, "in point of fact, the quarter tablet willn't keep you, well, so to speak, *erect*, Father, for the hour or so most men will want." "Nevermind your hour or erection," the priest says, "I just want it so I won't piss on my shoes."

The two men laugh.

SEAN: Nevermind the hour or erection is right! True for him. But I know the pain of pissing on my shoes.

E. J.: It's true for you.

SEAN: And true all the same there's a good few priests around the country didn't need Viagra for the auld erection. They're getting their comeuppance now I'd say.

E. J.: Faith, they're under pressure with years. That's for sure. Hadn't ye the same thing over, Sean? In Boston and California and those places?

SEAN: The very same, Godhelpus, one side of the country to the other, priests and bishops and would you believe, most all of them Irish, all over the papers there a few years ago, and millions spent paying the claims, and millions more before it's over I suppose. They had to sell the archbishop's mansion in Boston and the new man—a Capuchin—took an apartment in town and the old one—Bernie Law—off to Rome for a cushy job in the Vatican, out of harm's way, as it were.

E. J.: You can be sure the bishops are the prime boys, Sean. Well able for trouble. Ach. The priests left out on the line to dry and the prime boys called back to headquarters. They must have a fairly big office in the Vatican—for the sacked bishops of Ireland and America.

SEAN: St. Peter's Principle.
E. J.: St. Peter's what?
SEAN: Promoted to their level of misfeasance.

They both laugh knowingly.

E. J.: St. Peter's Principle indeed. Now you've said it. And the likes of poor Fr. Callaghan below left holding the bag, trying to repair the damage, reading out letters every week at Mass, apologizing for some pedophile forty years ago, and no one giving him the pound or the pence, and he could have retired long go but for once he's gone there's no priest for three parishes out the peninsula. Ah, the bishops are prime boys, of that you can be sure. Company men, all secrecy and chicanery, then off to Rome when the going gets tough. Bailed out just like the bankers and exchequer. And the people without consolation and the good priests damaged and the country ruined because of it.
SEAN: The same way over. Things never are as they seem to be. There's always more to it than meets the eye. Who's to know who is to be believed?
E. J.: Will you stop. All bollix and codswallop. Scandal and recession. The Celtic Tiger hunted, Tiger Woods hunted. And a good few bishops hunted here last Christmas, after Judge Murphy's Dublin Report. The bishop of Limerick, half a dozen others. Sacked 'em all. And more or less good riddance to them. And blast 'em, the TD's and Taoiseach are all bravery and indignation and wasn't it them gave them power from the start? Dev and his crowd. Article 2? Turning on each other, it's a sight to behold, Sean, like rats on a sinking ship. Biggest thing since the Berlin Wall, or the fall of the U.S.S.R. or your 9-11. The end of the church in Holy Ireland.
SEAN: Much the same over, E. J.—the bishops and

politicos—always at each other over something.
Abortion or gay marriage. Torture or stem cells.
Last year it was Burke and O'Malley going at it over
Kennedy. Or more precisely over Kennedy's corpse.

E. J.: Sounds like a bar fight in Bunratty! Burke, O'Malley,
Kennedy . . . but what's the bother Sean? He's been dead
with years.

SEAN: Not the president, the senator. Last of the brothers,
Teddy, you know. The youngest of them, and the oldest,
Godhelpus.

E. J.: Yes, yes, what about it? He'd a mighty funeral. It was
in the TV. Didn't Obama give the eulogy?

SEAN: He did, of course, and buried at Arlington with the
brothers. Oh, the leaders of the world gave him his due,
fair play to them. And the citizens. It's the princes of the
church that had the quibble—one of them upbraiding
the other for opening the arms of the church to your
man, and him so famously a sinner.

E. J.: Yes, of course, that drowned woman. What's that they
called her? Chappaquiddick? Aren't we all sinners? Isn't
that in it? "All fallen short of the glory of God?"

SEAN: Kopechne, Mary Jo, the woman. Oh, they'd forgive
him that, and the divorce, and the drink and all that
carry on. But he voted with his caucus on abortion
rights.

E. J.: Still in all, he'd a tough enough time of it, the
poor cratur, his brothers slaughtered, his chances lost.
Give him his requiems, is the thing I say, and no more
about it.

SEAN: Of course, that's what the cardinal of Boston did,
E. J.—gave him the use of the church, met him at the
doors of the church, like any dead Catholic, shook the
holy water and incense and liturgies over the man's
corpse and blessed him on his way in the journey—the
corporal work of mercy we're all called to do.

E. J.: No less, no more. Saint and sinner alike, pope and

peasant, rich and poor. All the one in death, the great leveler.

SEAN: In point of fact, E. J., it's what's brought me banging at your door this morning. The auld leveler . . .

He picks up the canvas bag from its place on the chair in the corner and sets it on his knees and slowly reveals the contents of the bag by pushing the edges of the bag down around the base to reveal a pale marble colored sculpture of an angel.

E. J.: (*Not certain if it's a gift.*) Cripes, isn't it lovely. That's a dear thing. Is it marble, Sean?

SEAN: Not exactly. Can't travel with bronze or brass anymore. Airport security. Man-made. High-grade polymer. In actual fact, I suppose, a kind of plastic. "The Guardian Angel" is what they call it in the catalog.

E. J.: (*Thinking it might be a gift.*) From the duty free? You shouldn't've Sean. That's too much trouble. That's a dear thing.

SEAN: Well, not exactly, E. J. Well, in a way, I suppose . . . in actual fact, now, these would be the ashes, or else to say, more precisely, the urn in which the ashes of one Margaret Mary O'Hara, late of Atlantic City, New Jersey, are contained, and whose people have asked me could they be scattered in the sea on the west coast of Ireland.

E. J.: (*Startled, rising from his chair in shocked disbelief.*) For fook sake, Sean, there's been a dead woman's corpse in the room and we carrying on like a pair of eedgits about bishops and senators and pedophiles! Fook sake, Sean, you might've told me . . .

SEAN: Not exactly a corpse, E. J., but shall we say a greatly reduced version of her former self.

E. J.: Inside the angel? Her mortal remains?

SEAN: Her mortal remains, I suppose, now that you put it like that. Yes, I suppose that's right. The angel's hollow.

E. J.: (*Approaching the thing and scrutinizing it closely.*) Like the Cadbury eggs and Easter rabbits. Hollow on the inside. And a tidy job it makes of it, Sean. Very handy. And the bag to match?

SEAN: No, E. J., that's one of Mary's. She gave it to me to, well, "get a handle on it," so to speak.

E. J.: For fook sake, Sean. I never actually saw such a thing. It's all burial around here. As you know yourself. We'll all be in the fire soon enough.

SEAN: I'm sorry to have startled you, E. J.

E. J.: It's no bother, Sean. I'm a man who's been around plenty of corpses, only to say here it's more boxes and burials instead of cremated angels. You'd never find a crematorium in these parts. Not at all. Dublin or Cork, I suppose. And mostly Protestants or foreigners. Everybody here goes into the ground at Kilcrona or Moyarta or Kilballyowen or Lisheen. And, as we'd say, more or less "intact."

SEAN: And many's the grave you yourself has opened.

E. J.: Will you stop. I couldn't count them. It's the done thing. Shoulder and shovel work, mud and puddle, stone and clay. Neighbors do the job. Didn't I do it for the people in your own house in times gone by. Peg and Porrig, Godblessthem.

SEAN: And none does it better than E. J. O'Curry—the corporal work of mercy.

E. J.: Well, I've done my part. I'm not a professional man like yourself Sean, back in America, or Collins, below with his hearse and coffins, but here it's only what neighbors do—the digging of the grave—a last decency done to others as we expect will be done to us.

SEAN: I knew you'd be the man to assist me.

E. J.: (*Looking again at the plastic angel.*) Was she a smallish woman, Mrs. O'Hara?

SEAN: I couldn't tell you. I never met her. Or any of her people.

E. J.: And is that herself, then, I mean, a likeness of her? The face of an angel, the figure of her? And a fine shape she had.

SEAN: No, no, E. J., that's a production number, out of a catalog.

E. J.: Yes, yes, I see, Sean. All the same, it's a lovely thing, very . . . well, *angelic* I suppose you'd say, perched on the rocks there like at the edge of the cliff.

SEAN: I suppose there's a kind of comfort in it. To think of her looking down from heaven above.

E. J.: Like Jesus himself she was.

SEAN: How do you mean?

E. J.: Well, first she "descended into hell," that'd be the fire, and "on the third day" she "rose again from the dead, and then ascended into heaven where" she "sits at the right hand of the Father." Isn't that all in the Apostles' Creed?

SEAN: How well you have it, E. J. You could've been a priest.

E. J.: That's more of a mugs game . . . what could've been.

SEAN: So, you'll give me a hand then, with these duties?

E. J.: Ah sure, Sean, I make out that's a one-man job.

SEAN: It's not a thing that should be done alone . . .

E. J.: Scattering ashes?

SEAN: (*officiously*) The care and disposition of the dead.

E. J.: No, no, of course, you're right, the more—in a manner of speaking—the merrier. Isn't that the way of a proper wake?

SEAN: God knows, E. J. you've a way of "seeing things." "A great brain box" said Paddy Mullaney years ago. "The O'Curry breed!" Sure, you couldn't beat it. God knows, there is a science to everything.

E. J.: I suppose there's something to it after all.

SEAN: You'd know there is . . . bred in the bone.

E. J.: No, no, not the breeding, Sean, but the meaning of it . . . the church, the life of faith, the rubrics and rituals. There must be something to it, don't you think?

SEAN: Sure it's hard to know. Many's the time the old woman of my own house across the road, the Lord've mercy on her, as devout herself as Mother Teresa, every night on her knees with novenas and glorious and sorrowful mysteries, and every summer up in the bus to knock for the holy water and the apparitions and many's the night I would see her turning her palms to the fire and turning to me she would often say, "I wonder if there's anything at all. I wonder if he hears us when we pray." After everything, E. J., it was as much wonder as faith with her, as much doubt as certainty.

E. J.: Still, there must be something to it, Sean. The other side. Don't you think there's something to it? Otherwise why would people be at it all these years, going off in the bare feet, half starved, in all weathers, in hard times, off to Mass and making their stations and living saintly lives. Surely there must be something to it. Even if the bishops let us down. Is that all there is? You're dead and buried? Or dead and burned? There must be something more to it than that . . . don't you think, Sean?

SEAN: That's the blessed hope of the matter, E. J. We can only hope.

E. J.: (*Leaning close to the fire, speaking into it.*) Because in truth I can tell you Sean, many's the time I sensed my own dead, blessed mother here in the house, and she's gone with going on fifty years.

SEAN: Now, for you E. J., that'd tell you something.

E. J.: And my father, a man you knew yourself, Sean, God be good to him, below in the cow cabins, many's the time I'd find myself in some predicament, dosing a sick heifer, or up to my elbows trying to turn some poor cratur inside another, trying to bring it forth into the world and just when I think that the cow and the calf and myself will be killed with it, just when I'm perished with the pulling of it, it's as if the old man is suddenly at my shoulders and pulling with me and whispering softly in my ears, faith, Sean, I did often hear it: "Take heart, boy! Take it handy," and then with a gush and the calf is out . . . and I fallen backwards with the thing in my lap, laying in the hay and dung and splash of it, grinning heavenward, crazy with the miracle of it all.

SEAN: So maybe there's something to it, after all? Maybe we're all happily haunted by them that's gone before us? Is that what you'd say, E. J.?

E. J.: (*Turning from the fire.*) Come here to me Sean. Was she a holy woman? Mrs. O'Hara?

SEAN: I couldn't say, E. J., I never met her. All I know is that her family wanted, according to the letter that came with the angel, because I suppose it was a wish of hers made known to them . . . they wanted her ashes cast into the sea in the west of Ireland.

E. J.: Because she was from here, I suppose?

SEAN: I couldn't say. Or maybe her people. Devil if I know a thing about it.

E. J.: But where to do it? Off the cliff, behind? As we'd do with kittens, the wee shits, or puppies when the bitch has whelped? The bag into the briny deep job?

SEAN: Ah no, E. J., I thought we'd take a ride out the peninsula, along the estuary, the day is fine. My thought is that the right place will make itself known to us.

E. J.: Yes, yes . . . the right place . . .

SEAN: I'd say we'll know it when we see it.

E. J.: Yes, yes . . . when we see it . . .

SEAN: Will we make for the road then, E. J.?

E. J.: We should see Fr. Callaghan first, below.

SEAN: Fr. Callaghan?

E. J.: She was a Catholic woman, Mrs. O'Hara, wasn't she? You'd know by the name. And holy, I make out. Look at her there, Sean, the angel, Sean. You can see she was a good and decent sort. I make out she must've had devotions.

SEAN: Right, E. J. Of course, dead right, Fr. Callaghan, of course we should.

E. J.: I've to settle with him for my Easter duty.

SEAN: Two birds with the one stone, so. I could sort an offering.

E. J.: (*Putting on his cap and coat.*) C'mon Sean. We'll make for the road. (*Going out the door, he dips a finger in the holy water font and blesses himself.*)

SCENE 2

The interior of a small bungalow on the seafront at the edge of a small village on the Shannon Estuary. The office of the parish priest, Fr. Michael Callaghan, an elderly cleric. The room is a shamble of books and half-finished projects. Upstage center is a large writing desk littered with papers. It sits under the window that looks out onto the wide mouth of the River Shannon across to the hills of County Kerry. A castle stands at the end of the pier and a litter of small boats are tied to buoys. Fr. Callaghan is dressed in long underwear and a patchwork quilted bathrobe—like Joseph's coat of many colors—tied with blue baling rope, an unlikely cincture. He is wearing a pair of loose-fitting boots and nodding over a book in his wingback chair.

Two figures pass in front of the window. The doorbell rings off stage. Fr. Callaghan exits through a door in the upstage right corner, voices of greeting are heard off stage.

SEAN: Did we catch you napping, Father?
FR. CALLAGHAN: Not hardly, Sean. 'Twas a shower I was caught in, earlier the morning, and had to toss things in the dryer to be ready for Maundy Thursday Services this evening. Come in Sean. Who's that you have with you? Your infamous neighbor, Eamon Joe O'Curry?

The three men enter the room, Fr. Callaghan leading the way, clearing the books off of two of the chairs, setting them on top of other piles of books on the desk covered with books and papers. Sean follows carrying the canvas bag with the urn. E. J., curling his cap in his hands, follows behind them.

SEAN: Don't go to any bother Father. We willn't be long, no need to clear the chairs.

FR. CALLAGHAN: Not at all. Sit down, gentlemen. Excuse the ruins. Ever since Mrs. Morrisey . . .

E. J.: A woman brings great order to a place.

SEAN: Any hope of another housekeeper, Father?

FR. CALLAGHAN: Ah no . . . sure Annie'd been with me 40 years. Times are different now. You couldn't get someone to live like that. You're back again, Sean. How long have ye?

SEAN: The month I suppose, Father, if all goes well.

FR. CALLAGHAN: And how are things in Chicago? Anything strange since we saw you last? No jihadis or terrorists?

E. J.: Like all the king's horses and all the king's men . . . the unbearable whiteness of Trumpism.

FR. CALLAGHAN: (*sighing, resigned*) God knows, the poor world's a sad and broken place.

E. J.: A sad and broken place, indeed. We're on a bit of a mission, Father.

FR. CALLAGHAN: I see, said the blind man, when he couldn't see at all.

E. J.: Actually a pair of missions. First, I've to do the Easter duty.

FR. CALLAGHAN: Between the stirrup and the ground, mercy sought and mercy found. Sure, E. J. willn't the general absolution do? Shortage of priests, and Easter coming. (*He rises from his chair, stands before E. J.*) "Absolvu te, et cetera, et cetera . . . go and sin some more."

E. J.: (*In a low embarrassed voice with his head bowed.*) Fair dues to you, Father. (*He reaches in his pocket and pulls out a small wad of bank notes and places them on the desk. The priest wordlessly covers them with one of the books.*)

FR. CALLAGHAN: Aren't you very good, Eamon Joe. (*He blesses the bowed head of the supplicant. Touches his shoulder.*

Clears his throat and changes tone.) And the other matter, lads?

SEAN: Having to do with, well, mortal remains. (*He slips the angel from the canvas bag.*)

FR. CALLAGHAN: (*Crossing himself and catching his breath.*) Dear mother of God . . . a mission, indeed.

E. J.: Sean's brought them with him from America. They're to be scattered. In the Shannon, Father. The woman's wishes.

FR. CALLAGHAN: And what woman would that be, precisely?

SEAN: Margaret Mary O'Hara, Father, late of Atlantic City, New Jersey. At least we know it to be her family's wishes. (*Sean hands an envelope, containing a letter and a bank draft, to the priest.*) You will see I've been given the undertaking—to scatter the remains in the River Shannon, in the West of Ireland, and no more about it.

FR. CALLAGHAN: Pity that angel couldn't fly here on its own. (*He laughs in advance at his own joke.*) That would be "urning" its keep! (*He laughs again.*)

E. J.: Fair play to you, Father. (*Looking at Sean.*) That's the man for the turning of phrases.

FR. CALLAGHAN: Better if I could've turned the spade. I wonder did either of you hear about poor Christy Callan?

E. J.: Christy Callan? No, I didn't? (*Acting the straight man.*) Was he from around these parts, Father?

FR. CALLAGHAN: I suppose he was from over Doonbeg side. He was nearing the ninety and long married and very much at the end of his tether, bedridden I suppose, "in extremis." And he wakes to the smell of his favorite chocolate chip cookies wafting through the house and he wonders has he died and gone to heaven. So he gathers what's left of his will and resources, climbs out of the bed, hobbles himself into the kitchen and there on the table, cooling on newspapers are several dozen freshly baked cookies. Says he to himself, either I'm dead and gone to heaven, or at the very least, the wife of these long years has made me these to soften the sadness of my impending doom. He reaches one of his long, bony hands in the direction of the cookies when out of nowhere comes the spatula to slap it back and his wife's giving out with, "leave those alone, Christy, they're for the funeral!"

(*He laughs again.*) Now for you!

E. J.: Will you stop! But that's a good one. Leave 'em alone. For the funeral! (*He feigns more laughter than is due.*)

SEAN: You have them all, Father. Every one of them.

(*Laughs politely and sets the angel back down on the radiator.*)

FR. CALLAGHAN: Now lads, what was it we were talking about?

E. J.: A blessing, Father, on the ashes, before we . . .

SEAN: A kind of final commendation . . .

FR. CALLAGHAN: Yes, yes, I see, the hail and farewell. Well, in point of fact, now Sean, in point of actual fact, you see, the Holy Father does not approve, as it were, of "scattering" per se. He'd prefer we bury the remains. Intact, in fact.

E. J.: Why's that I wonder?

FR. CALLAGHAN: Ah sure, I suppose it has to do with the resurrection on the last day.

SEAN: You mean the dead can be raised to life, but the scattered cannot be reconstituted?

FR. CALLAGHAN: Well . . . I'm sure there's more to it than . . .

E. J.: But what about the holy relics? Aren't the saints fairly scattered—in bits and pieces—around the churches of the world? Joan of Arc. Wasn't she burned at the stake? And John Bosco? And what about your man, Oliver Plunkett above in Drogheda? His head in the tabernacle in the side altar. Where's the rest of him? Under the altar stones of a hundred parishes? Where will he be on the last day?

FR. CALLAGHAN: Of course that'd be beyond my own
ecclesiastical pay grade, E. J.

E. J.: Sure, Father, you could teach the bishops a thing
or two.

FR. CALLAGHAN: Preaching to bishops—old Canon
Grace used to say—like farting at skunks. You'll win
some battles but you'll lose the war.

SEAN: All the more so the higher ye go.

FR. CALLAGHAN: How do you mean, Sean?

SEAN: Like crapping at pachyderms by the time you get to
the bishop of Rome.

The three men fall into embarrassed laughter.

E. J.: Couldn't beat the Yanks for a way with words.

FR. CALLAGHAN: Like crapping at pachyderms. I'll
remember that.

SEAN: Well, here's the thing Father, I'm a working man
and I'm on the job and whatever His Holiness says, I've
promised these folks that the job will be done. That
letter they sent me gives me full authority. (*He nods
towards the envelope the priest is holding. The priest tilts his
glasses to read the thing.*)

FR. CALLAGHAN: "We the undersigned do hereby
authorize and instruct . . . scattered in the River
Shannon . . . earliest possible convenience . . . in
accordance with . . . permanent thanks. . . ." Everything
in order there, Sean, signed and sealed. (*He holds the
smaller piece of paper aloft to look at it.*) And what have we
here?

SEAN: That's a check in the amount of three hundred
dollars, made out to me, apparently for services
rendered. Of course, we never discussed a fee, and I had
no charges for them, it was only something I agreed
to do because their funeral director in New Jersey
was a friend of mine, Brian McNamara. Met him at a
convention once, and he knew that I was back and forth

here and when he heard what they wanted, well, one thing followed on the other.

E. J.: As they do.

FR. CALLAGHAN: As they do, indeed.

SEAN: Of course to me it's just the corporal work of mercy, no bother, no trouble, no charge, et cetera. I wouldn't feel right about taking the money, so I more or less decided that I'd endorse the check to whomever it was said the final prayers over Mrs. O'Hara. Which is why, of course, Father, we came to you.

FR. CALLAGHAN: Yes, yes, I quite understand. The corporal work of mercy, yes. Be a good man, E. J., hand me my book.

E. J. looks on the desk for the lectionary and passes it over to the priest who opens it to the proper pages.

FR. CALLAGHAN: In the name of the Father and of the Son and of the Holy Ghost . . .

SEAN *rising* and E. J. *kneeling on one knee*: Amen . . .

FR. CALLAGHAN: Let us pray . . .

All three men fall into a prayerful posture and countenance as the priest carries on with the obsequies.

SCENE 3

The interior of a small pub on the seafront at the western end of the peninsula—The Lighthouse Inn. A broad window looks out from the upstage center on to the esplanade and estuary. Lourda Kearney, a fetching redhead in her middle forties, is the widowed proprietress and publican. She stands behind the crescent of a dark hardwood bar at stage right trying to tune in the radio. The wind is howling. She cannot find a good station. She crosses the room and puts coals in the fire, opposite the bar, stage left center, and crossing back, tightens the shawl around her shoulders. She

*returns to her place behind the bar. She looks off into the middle
distance in meditation. She catches her breath. She seems somehow
in deep reverie, on the edge of tears. The noise of a car engine out
of doors, two car doors slamming, the noise of which shakes her
from her reverie. Two figures pass in front of the window and
enter from the door upstage left: E. J. and Sean, their faces and
clothing covered with dust, enter, brushing themselves off, not very
successfully. E. J. is carrying the plastic angel.*

E. J.: God bless all here.
LOURDA: The living and the dead.
SEAN: God bless the house and the mistress of it.
LOURDA: Now, Sean, you're very welcome! Not so many
     Yanks come this far out the west. And who's the white-
     faced pilgrim you've brought with ye? And what's he
     got with him? The angel of mercy or of mischief? Is it
     Easter or Halloween he's done up for? All Saints or April
     Fools? Ghost or goblin? Trick or treat? Rogue or Easter
     rabbit? Hard to know. Either way you're welcome, the
     two of ye.
E. J.: (*Setting the empty angel urn on the bar upstage right, he
     seats himself on a corner stool facing downstage. Still wiping
     his arms, taking off his cap, running his hands through his
     hair, stamping his feet.*) Give us whiskey Missus. Paddy
     whiskey. I'm fairly shook with mortuary duties we're
     after doing.
LOURDA: St. Patrick's holy water, then. That'd be the
     usual.
SEAN: (*to E. J.*) I thought you said we'd say nothing about
     it. "Present nothing to anyone"—your very words.
E. J.: There's no fear for Lourda Kearney. She's an honest
     woman. And all too well schooled in the tears of things.
     A tough old life, and well she knows it. Whiskey,
     Lourda! I'm nearly perished. "*Sunt lacrimae rerum et
     mentem mortalia tangunt,*" and wasn't it true for them.
LOURDA: (*Drawing a double shot from the upturned bottle*

hanging behind her.) Now, E. J. your *spirits.* Nothing but the top shelf. And for you, Sean?

SEAN: (*Dusting himself, wiping his face.*) A coffee, Lourda, thank you, I'm driving and jet-lagged. (*He places a bank note on the bar.*) He'll want another, I'd say, sooner than later.

LOURDA: And what brings the two of you out to the west from the quiet townland I grew up in?

E. J.: (*Gulping the first double whiskey in a hurry.*) The corporal works of mercy. (*Tapping the empty glass on the bar.*) Have you another of those, missus?

SEAN: We're on the job, Lourda. I was given an undertaking by a colleague in New Jersey who knows I'm always coming and going.

LOURDA: The here-today and gone-tomorrow Yank. No bother to ye, Sean. Since I was a child and longer, maybe.

SEAN: He asked if I'd bring the ashes of a woman to scatter them. We're after doing the job, E. J. and me.

LOURDA: Oh, I see. Hard duties, done then. Was she from here, I wonder? Had she a connection to these parts?

SEAN: I couldn't tell you. They weren't too precise. Just that it was her hope to be scattered near the "banks of the River Shannon" according to the funeral director. They shipped her to me in this angel urn, with a letter, "To Whom It May Concern," et cetera, which authorized me to possess, transport, and properly dispose, et cetera. All signed and notarized. And a check, made out to me, in the amount of three hundred, though I'd never charge them for the job. More than happy to accommodate. But as it worked out, it was just as well.

E. J.: Fr. Callaghan's the man who got the dosh. For the holy rites and courtesies. (*Mimicking the cleric's voice.*) "You never said, Sean, those were *Catholic* ashes."

LOURDA: (*Laughing along.*) The auld "currency exchange and conversion!"

E. J.: All the same, a good job he made of it, give him his due.

LOURDA: A great one for praying, in fairness. The cratur.

E. J.: Still, it was Sean and me who went the distance with her.

LOURDA: Good man for ye.

SEAN: Such as we're given to do.

E. J.: And got a gob full of her dust to dust and ashes to ashes blown back at us for our troubles. Give me another whiskey, missus.

LOURDA: (*Scrutinizing the dust on their jacket sleeves, ignoring the drink order.*) Godhelpus, E. J.

E. J.: Sean there, bending to the task of it, me at his shoulder, in the middle of the prayers and ejaculations. "*Miserere mei, Deus* . . ." A sudden updraft of air and he dumping the angel. And we're made up like a pair of circus clowns. I make out she'll be back in Jersey tomorrow, counting on the tide to do its part.

LOURDA: Like Aer Lingus, itself.

E. J.: Sean said as much to the next of kin when he called him from his phone from the scene. (*Downing the last of his second whiskey. Tapping the glass on the counter.*) Now, missus.

SEAN: Pace yourself, E. J. what's the panic? Amn't I driving? Haven't we time?

LOURDA: He's wanting to put up a little store against Good Friday tomorrow. And the pubs closed and the priests open for business.

E. J.: (*Beginning to roar a little with the drink.*) Whiskey, missus! Can you deliver?

LOURDA: I'm bolting the door myself before long now. I've places to go and things to do.

SEAN: (*Tendering another ten euro note.*) Lourda.

LOURDA: (*Turning to draw another shot from the bottle.*)

Wasn't it very decent of ye two, just the same, to see her final wishes carried out. And she a perfect stranger to the two of ye.

E. J.: Least we could do. No less than we'd all want for ourselves. All of us need someone in the end, to see us on our final journey.

LOURDA: (*Catching her breath, bowing her head, her arm still up, holding the glass to the shot dispenser of the upturned bottle, the whiskey running over the glass and running down her arm. As if a weakness comes upon her, with her other hand behind her, she braces herself between the bar and bottle and groans deeply as if punched in the gut.*) Oh, God. . . . Oh, Gabriel.

E. J.: (*Tenderly, knowing.*) Forgive me, Lourda, I never . . .

SEAN: (*In a similar voice.*) Godhelpus, Lourda.

LOURDA: (*Regaining some of her composure.*) You're all right lads. It's OK. It's only some days it's so very lonesome, even these years since.

E. J.: Sure, Lourda, you're only right to miss him.

SEAN: It's only natural, the tears of things. Only natural.

LOURDA: (*Weeping quietly, in control.*) And I'd've shuttered and sold this place years ago, only for the hope that his sweet self might reappear or the corpse of him might wash up on the strand outside and come looking for me. That's why I could never leave. These ten years since he disappeared, like Cuchulain off the Loop, pursued by dogs of love and grief, to death.

E. J.: Oh, Lourda, I'm sorry.

LOURDA: And where was Fr. Callaghan that time? Never a mention of a Mass, or a month's mind, never a word of it. Because there was no corpse? Because he thought he might have killed himself? Or because he knew it was the church that damaged Gabriel, hounded by it all his whole life?

E. J.: Come here to me, Lourda, you needn't rehearse old . . .

SEAN: Hush, E. J., let her be.

LOURDA: And poor sweet Gabriel, a lovely, blue-eyed angel himself at twelve and serving Mass and the curate asking, "would he like to be in the passion play . . . ?"

E. J.: Time heals all wounds, dear Lourda . . . will you give me whiskey, Lourda.

She pulls from behind the bar a full bottle of her finest whiskey, fills his glass and leaves the bottle on the bar.

LOURDA: The beloved apostle, that's what he'd be. Washed Gabriel's feet, the priest did. Giving out with Latin the whole time. That's how it started, poor Gabriel, and him not thirteen, not even knowing the way of his body . . . maybe he sensed in it something wrong, the way as how it maybe pleasured him. He was only a boy, and maybe not so much the way he was touching him, but the way it made him feel—excited, tickled, comforted, who's to know?

SEAN: Latin? Lourda?

LOURDA: "*Mandatum novum do vobis . . .*"

E. J.: (*Sadly, slowly.*) I give you a new mandate . . . a new commandment . . .

LOURDA: that ye love one another . . .

E. J.: as I have loved you.

LOURDA: (*Sobbing wretchedly. Holding herself. Bent over in grief.*) Oh God and we did, we loved one another, he was such a fine husband. A lovely man. The way he'd hold me. I miss him so. And no trace of his body these seven years since. So that some days I wonder is he gone at all? Or only gone from me?

E. J.: Steady, missus . . . Godhelpus, it's sad.

LOURDA: It's a cruel thing not to have the body back, to cast back into the sea itself, or the grave, or the fire—it hardly matters. What only matters is we go to the edge of it with them, as you're after saying, Eamon Joe, see

them on their way . . . the way you did with that woman
today.

SEAN: And was it how the priest tampered with him? Was
it that, as you say, "hounded" him, Lourda?

LOURDA: Sure, Sean, I couldn't tell you. Things aren't
always as they seem. There was never any mention of
that. Nor any bit of strangeness about him, the way with
him, I mean, our intimate life. Nothing but tenderness
and true communion. So very generous, he was. Almost
holy, the way he touched me (*she catches her breath*) and I
shouldn't be telling you any of this . . .

E. J.: (*Shaken by the disclosures of private matters.*) Oh,
Lourda . . . let me pour you a drink. (*He downs his
whiskey and pours another.*)

SEAN: Sure, you're OK, Lourda, have no fear.

LOURDA: But he made me feel *holy*, no other word for
it, to be with him, Sean, almost sacramental. Behold,
he would say, when he'd catch me naked, I show you a
mystery—and I could tell he would give me anything,
everything . . .

E. J.: (*Embarrassed, incredulous, more than a little drunk.*)
Body and blood, soul and divinity. (*He considers the figure
of the angel urn and runs his hand along the curves of the
sculpted angel.*)

LOURDA: And then he changed. As if the light went out of
him.

SEAN: Did he say what it was?

LOURDA: I could never draw it out of him, but the
change came over him years ago, when the first scandals
were reported in the papers. The light went out of
him. And it wasn't so much the priests—hardly more
than boys themselves, he'd often say, when they went
into seminary, the way every family pushed one of the
sons, the sickly one, or the second one, or the one who
might've been a little artful . . . they would have pressed
Gabriel, but for his music, always at the piano and tin

whistle, anything he picked up, he'd make music out of.
God knows, for years it was just a certain way of getting
an education and a job with a pension.

SEAN: What's that they say? "Vocations follow famine."

E. J.: God knows we never had a shortage of those. And
who but the priests kept the people going in those times.
Wasn't Fr. Meehan and his ark out on the strand outside
at low tide to read the Mass when none was permitted,
in penal days. And the Soupers and landlords and
Marcus Keane, blast him, the landlord's agent. And the
children of these parishes scattered to the far corners of
the earth. But for the faith and the holy fathers, where
would any of them be?

SEAN: A poor country that couldn't feed its own, my
grandfather always said. It's why he never would come
back. Though he pined for his home-place until the day
he died—a prison guard in Jackson, Michigan. Maybe
the same for Margaret Mary O'Hara. Let down by the
home she loved, her heart turned against the land of
heart's desire. Who's to know?

E. J.: Them that left could never return. Them that stayed
could never get away. At least Margaret Mary, the cratur,
found her way home. (*He runs a finger along the cheekbone
of the angel.*)

LOURDA: (*Sobbing.*) It was the church that my poor
Gabriel loved, down on his knees every night at his
rosary, making his first Fridays and novenas, fasting and
praying through the holy seasons, never missing a Mass
or mission. Playing every Sunday and teaching the choir,
singing his heart out. "Who sings prays twice," he would
always tell me. His fine tenor voice. Even just speaking,
it was music to me. It was not what the priests did, but
what the bishops didn't do.

E. J.: Never mind the bishops, Lourda, have a drink.
(*He pours himself another and returns to his fondling of
the angel.*)

LOURDA: The way they betrayed the people. Shifting abusers from one place to the next. Company men. All hush and secrets. Out for the church, not the people. It tampered badly with him, poor Gabriel. And after he'd turned his heart and soul and his art over to them as a boy. He saw them for the phonies that they were. And it soured something sweet and pristine in him. Hushed him altogether.

SEAN: Because he stopped believing?

E. J.: (*Growing more intoxicated, slurring his words.*) I have fought the good fight, I have kept the faith. (*Wryly.*) But I've not finished the course as of yet! (*Pouring more.*) Give me whiskey, I tell you, that'll make me sing!

LOURDA: Because it took the mystery away, the language he'd learned to speak to God in. What had seemed divine now seemed somehow depraved. He'd come out of the church on Sundays muttering, "sounding brass and tinkling cymbals," oh, it damaged him, hollowed him out like that poor plastic angel and robbed him of his sense of things. And all the sweet things that used to pleasure us turned joyless, meaningless, dark, and sad. The light, I tell you, was going out of him. So what could I tell old Michael Callaghan, when he came nosing around after here Gabriel's disappearance, with his "had he shown any signs of melancholy or despair?" What could I tell him?

E. J.: (*Stupourous.*) Never cross a priest, that's what my father said, years 'go, Godblesshim. They do be wicked when you rise them . . .

LOURDA: That after months of a darkening spiral, Gabriel woke one April morning, Gabriel stood from his tea, grabbed his fishing pole and his tackle of ribbons and sinkers and said, "I'm going out to get some mackerel for the dinner." And truth told it seemed very early for mackerel to me, but the way he hugged me, and pressed me to him, and for the first time in months, after

that godawful winter, there seemed a lightness to him,
a kind of ease, and I was glad just to see him going out
again and so what could I tell Michael Callaghan at all
when he asked if I thought Gabriel would hurt himself?
How could I know? And I still don't know, Sean, there's
the terror of it, I still don't know the meaning of it all,
only that he's gone from me and I'm waiting ever since,
in a kind of limbo, neither saved nor damned, certain
of one thing or another, afraid that the dead still walk
among us and afraid they don't. Afraid I might see my
poor Gabriel again, afraid I won't.

SEAN: Had he lost his faith?

LOURDA: Ah, no, but his religion, his *language* of faith, his
voice, his song. And that is what hounded him over the
edge, that poor wingless angel of a man I loved. I *love*.
Whether he went out there and was swept up by a freak
wave, or swept off the edge by the wind, or leapt off
the edge on his own—either way, it was the church that
pushed him and them that won't forgive him and them
that wants no part of him now.

SEAN: Godhelpus Lourda, the poor man. You poor, dear
woman . . .

E. J.: (*Drunk and perturbed.*) Never mind all that, Lourda,
have a drink, bring us whiskey, Sean, you'll have one
yourself! Put away all that other. No more about it.
Enough, I tell you. Never spare the night's feast for the
morning. There's a store in heaven that was never open.

LOURDA: Maybe that's a store that'll never close. But this
one does. Time now, lads, drink up. I've things to do.

E. J.: (*Drunkenly howling.*) Will you not give me something
for the road, missus? A last sup? Something to brace
me against tomorrow? Be an angel, Lourda, haven't
we always been neighbors and friends? (*Petting the
angel, speaking to it.*) Is that all there is then? An empty
promise? A vacant grave? A hollow angel? Is there no
tomorrow? Are we all alone?

LOURDA: Time now, E. J. Time. Enough.

SEAN: I'm sorry, Lourda. I'll take him home.

LOURDA: Ah, sure, he's harmless, the cratur. Pure honest, the poor man. He's only looking, like the rest of us.

She takes up the angel urn in the corner, turns it over, unscrews the cap in the bottom and pours the remaining whiskey from the bottle into it. Fastens the cap back into place and places it in E. J.'s arms.

LOURDA: Now, for you, E. J. She's full of spirits. So, take your guardian angel home with you, Eamon Joe. She'll keep you warm, I'd say, and give you dreams. And put up with your howling.

E. J.: God bless you missus, the Lord spare ye. We'll go now, Sean, our Easter duties done!

SEAN: (*Standing. Leaving a banknote on the bar. Putting E. J.'s cap on his head.*) We'll go E. J., now, mind your angel, don't let her fall. It'd break her.

LOURDA: (*Sighing.*) We falling, broken angels, God bless us all . . .

The men leave by the door upstage left. Lourda puts the note in the till, wipes the bar, turns out the light and watches the shadows in the dark outside the window. God bless all here.

E. J.: (*Offstage, calling out.*) The living and the dead!

THE END

Chapter Fifteen

Shilling Life

Mostly I remember the quick pearlescent cloud, the milky stain it made in the rush of current, when I dumped Hughie's ashes in the water. And watching what remained of him disappear downstream, the thing that I thought of was that thing they said whenever the big music gathered and the masked man rode off at the end of that cowboy show I watched as a boy, "A fiery horse, with the speed of light and a cloud of dust, and a hearty 'Hi-Yo Silver, Away!' The Lone Ranger!"

There goes Hughie now, I thought, that big music racing in my brain. Hi-Yo Silver, Away!

The little bone fragments, bits and pieces of him, glistened in the gravel bed of the Water of Leith whilst his cloud of dust quickly worked its way in the current downstream to the eventual river mouth and out, I supposed, into the Firth of Forth and the North Sea and the diasporic waters of the world. I dipped the little metal disc I'd picked out of his ashes in the water, washing the dust of him off of it and held it up like a silver bullet. "Who was that masked man?" I said to myself and slipped it into my pocket with the other foreign coins.

I wiped my eyes and focused on the water. I was not weeping but I could feel it—like abundance, overflow, spillage, real.

I pulled a camera from my pocket and snapped a photo on the off chance that any of his family would want to see the little waterfall and the leafy banks of the river tucked into the west end of the distant city that had become, if not his final resting place, his launching place, his headwaters.

In my notebook I wrote, "13 August 2000, dumped Hugh MacSwiggan's ashes in the Waters of Leith near Dean Parish Church and Cemetery, Edinburgh," whether for the file back at the office or my own uncertain purposes, it's hard to say. I'd only started carrying a notebook again in the weeks since Hughie died. For the first time in years I was keeping track of things again, making notes, writing down oddments and loose ends. Hi-Yo Silver, Away!

I crossed back over the river by Dean Path and Bell's Brae, to Queensferry Street and left at Hope where I tossed the black plastic box I'd brought him in into a public barrel, then happened into Charlotte Square where a little crowd was gathering for the Edinburgh Book Festival—a tent city of the literati. The greensward was filling with bookish-looking sorts—women wearing eyeglasses and fashionable scarfs, men with straw hats and briefcases, and around the edges of the green, large tents turned into performance spaces, as if a traveling circus had arrived. Under one, J. K. Rowling was reading from her latest Harry Potter. The crowd of young teens, preteens, and their parents spilled from the tent onto the lawn. In another, according to the chalkboard sign, the feminist Andrea Dworkin was holding forth from her book called *Scapegoat: The Jews, Israel and Women's Liberation*. In another, a local poet was reading to a small but rapt audience—I listened in but couldn't make out his meaning, his accent was so thick, the images so dense. I browsed the bookstalls, bought nothing, had tea in the mirror-walled Spiegeltent, where I think I might have seen

Salman Rushdie holding forth for a TV crew. The life of fiction—I said to myself—the life of poetry. But I was neither artist nor aficionado. I was a tourist, passing through, my promise to old Hughie kept, suddenly glad for the ticket I kept in my pocket and the home, such as it was, and the life, such as it was, I would be returning to.

I left the square, walking up Rose Street, smiling at diners in the outdoor eateries, tossing coins in the hats of the buskers and jugglers and street magicians, making my way without agenda. At the end I turned right and stopped at the Scott Monument before walking down Princes Street through the throngs of revelers and shoppers and souvenir stalls and into St John the Evangelist at the corner of Lothian. It was a spot Hughie had marked on his map. According to the banner over the entrance to the church, a "Festival of Peace and Silence" was going on inside and I walked in and through that vaulted space among the contemplatives spread among the pews, apparently feasting on peace and silence, until I heard a low din of voices coming from a small room behind the sanctuary. It was the meeting Hughie had directed me to. I went in, put the pound note in the basket, sat down, listened in, and said my piece. An hour later, emerging from that great kirk's interior to the sound of pipers and drummers from the castle above, and the midafternoon's late season light washing over the swarm of glad-faced humanity, the ancient city in its August festivities, I felt, inexplicably, alive and well. I actually felt it. There was this emergent pang of longing for voices I knew. I wanted to tell them I was better now and coming home and hoped they would still be there when I returned. I looked for a phone to call home on.

I owed it to Hughie, I suppose, to go the distance with him. He'd gone some distances with me since I'd met him thirty years before when I was laid up in the hospital. Fractured hip and pelvis, broken leg and ankle, a couple of compressed vertebrae—I'd fallen from a third-story fire escape. I was hung over and doped up, in casts and traction, and lucky by all accounts to be alive after a party in my rented rooms near the university. It was an old apartment house where I'd been out on the fire escape, a rickety old wooden structure, acting the dark and moody artist, part Dylan Thomas, part Bob Dylan, with my bottle of J.W. Dant Kentucky sour mash, the first clear autumn evening after two weeks of rain.

And it was Eileen Doyle who I was trying to impress and Eileen's chest I was hoping to get ahold of and the J.W. Dant I could, of course, blame it on, on the better than even chance that Eileen demurred. That was my plan. After naming a couple of the constellations, and saying something memorable, maybe quoting Theodore Roethke or Emily Dickinson, and taking a swig from the bottle of bourbon, I'd begun my advances on lovely Eileen.

She was beautiful and I wanted her to be impressed by the up-and-coming man of letters I was fashioning myself to be. I had a few chords on a guitar and could sing some Leonard Cohen tunes as backup. I had the whiskey to boot. I knew some poems.

And it was J. Doggett Whitacker from West Virginia, our English professor, the son-of-a-bitch, who came out through the window, out onto the fire escape and began turning Eileen's sweet attentions away from me with his syrupy talk about the lost sister of the Pleiades, then the moon and its phases and the tides, and time—the mystery of it all, et-fecking-cetera. I could see in the way she was looking at him, and listening, and the smile widening on her face, that my chances for getting a hand on her breasts were disappearing with every silky thing he said in that sappy Southern accent of his, done up to sound professorial. So I stood up and cleared my throat and leaning back on the rail to say something unforgettably manful, though I can't for the life of me remember now, I must've leaned too heavily, or the rail was badly constructed, or maybe it was all those recent rains, the rotting wood gone soggy and all; whatever it was, the rail gave way and before I knew it I could feel myself falling backwards through the midair, falling into the oblivion of God only knows what peril, falling, falling.

It still always happens in slow motion. I can see the panic widening in Eileen's eyes and Doggett the son-of-a-bitch is trying to remain composed and I think there's a little Hollywood grin on my face, as if to say to him, "top this one, asshole," and I remember thinking I should push myself off, like those high divers in the movies do, the better to get an extra moment in the air to figure out exactly what I'm going to do next. And who could blame me for playing for time, even in my memory of it. Because—and I'm thinking all of this in slow motion—there's an awful lot of wires I could get tangled in and strangled or beheaded or electrocuted by, and there are those cement cellar steps at the back of the house to crack my head on like a water-damn-melon, and there's this brick barbeque pit back there somewhere and even missing all of those I'll probably break my neck just from the thirty-five, maybe forty-five feet of it all. This is an old house with high ceilings divided into cheap student apartments and I'm falling off of it. All these mangling, paralyzing, man-killing contingencies out there in the not-too-distant future—and before I can list all of them or calculate my odds of death or survival or recall the only item I retained from Physics 101 about bodies in motion and at rest, how they fall at thirty-two feet per second, squared; before I can wrap myself in the comfy bufferings of such contemplations—the notion of a second, squared, for example, or of falling bodies, or that look, part amazement, part regret, in lovely Eileen Doyle's eyes—I hit whatever's down there, must be the ground, left foot first, snapping that ankle and tibia, then right hip, fracturing that, then the rest of me, crashing into then coming to rest on the unflinching earth which is moving like every other star or moon through the mystery of time fecking-cetera. I'm flat on my back and looking up into it all, the vast basilica of the heavens. I'm seeing stars. And then I can feel myself rolling over, knees and elbows, then arms outstretched, assuming the all-fours, and I can't, for the life of me, get my breath. I can see myself, sort of out-of-body, as if occupying a balcony seat to this whole daft theater. There I am on all fours in the backyard, having missed all the fatal possibilities and if I could only get a break here, get a breath, I might not die, and then, after what seems a very long time, the wind that was flushed out of me when I hit is miraculously restored in one great intake and out-roaring moan, and I roll over on my back and look up at the stars. And I'm seeing every one of them with new appreciation, the millions and maybe billions of them in the firmament, and then suddenly, the faces of Professor Whitacker, that tweedy son-of-a-bitch, and Eileen Doyle and half a dozen other revelers and it's Whitacker, in that syrupy talk of his, who keeps shouting, "Did you hit your head, man, did you hit your head?" No doubt he figured I'd be an imbecile ever after and his conquest of Eileen Doyle would be more the cake-walk, what with myself, drooling and diapered and out of the picture.

"Who is the president of the United States?" he is shouting at me. "Who wrote 'The Love Song of J. Alfred Prufrock'? Do you know where you are? What day is it? Can you say your name?"

To assure him and the gathering retinue that, though damaged in some yet to be determined ways, my intellect and sensibilities remained intact, I began reciting "Who's Who," word for word, a piece I'd memorized for just such an occasion—not The Fall, as I later came to call it, but for the likes of Eileen Doyle with eyes such as hers and her perfect skin and her fine round breasts and clear autumn evenings under the stars and the hopes we all have of intimacy.

It was, by all accounts, a stirring recital, perfectly paced and delivered, in the fashionably beleaguered diction of the artist I imagined myself, at the time, to be:

A shilling life will give you all the facts:
How Father beat him, how he ran away,
What were the struggles of his youth, what acts
Made him the greatest figure of his day:

I could see the fright in their eyes giving way to wonder,
then amazement, that here I was in this epic pose, having
taken a dive, albeit inadvertently, that would have killed
ninety-nine out of every hundred ordinary men; and yet
here I was reciting sonnets to allay their worries, a man of
parts and substance to the end.

Of how he fought, fished, hunted, worked all night
Though giddy, climbed new mountains, named a sea:
Some of the last researchers even write
Love made him weep his pints like you and me.

And then pausing for the stanza's break, sighing slightly,
turning serious, turning my gaze ever so meaningfully,
looking deeply into Eileen's eyes as she hovered above me, I
eased the poem's little dagger home:

With all his honors on, he sighed for one
Who, say astonished critics, lived at home;
Did little jobs about the house with skill
And nothing else; could whistle; would sit still
Or potter round the garden; answered some
Of his long marvelous letters but kept none.[1]

In the slow motion I always remember this, tears are
welling in Eileen's eyes, those rhymes still sounding in her
tiny ivory ears, her bosom is heaving and she is holding my
hand between her breasts and wiping my face with her other
hand and Doggett Whitacker is looking utterly vanquished,
while the constellations are turning above them all, in the
bright firmament of heaven. But in the real-life version,

thirty years ago, I no more had Auden's memorable iambs out when I began to puke—all of that god-awful bourbon and, I believe, the remnants of a pepperoni pizza—projectile vomiting I think they call it, *Gone with the Wind* turned *Exorcist*—and the last thing I remember before blacking out was the look of horror or disgust in Eileen's eyes. I did not know her well enough to know.

And isn't that always the rub? Between the facts of the matter and the way we keep trying to wrestle them into compliance with our remembrance of them? Hardly one for "little jobs around the house," Eileen went to work with the State Department, managed several of the country's more difficult embassies, and resigned to head up an NGO doing relief work in the Congo. Doggett Whitacker moved West, became chair of the department at a small college, and wrote a novel that became a movie that was nominated for an Oscar. Their "long marvelous letters" and my own, lost in the mail as they always are.

As for me, I never became a rock star or poet, never had "all my honors on" or authored much of anything. My father never beat me. I never ran away. He drove his Lincoln into a bridge abutment one winter night on the way home, and spent two years paralyzed below the waist before he died, grateful there'd been no other cars involved.

"Christ," he'd always say, "they'd've sued us for a fortune."

I stayed home, did not become the doctor he wanted nor the lawyer he wanted nor the writer or rock star I always imagined myself. I married the Methodist minister's daughter and we went into business doing lawn maintenance and snow removal. Early morning work for the most part, it left my afternoons and evenings free. Through my father-in-law, who served on the township board, I got contracts to keep the grass mowed, the leaves cleaned up, and the roads clear of snow in the three township cemeteries. When the excavator who did their grave openings died, I bought his backhoe and took over. It was easy work and paid well enough and once folks started cremating more, I put a retort in and then another in the back of the pole barn where I stored my equipment. I hired some kids to do the heavy work—the backhoe and mower part of the business. When I couldn't find kids anymore, I hired Mexicans. I stayed around the office and took care of the cremations. The area morticians would send them over, in wooden caskets or cardboard boxes. I'd pull them from the hearse onto the push cart with the rollers, check out the paperwork to be sure everything was in order, all the permissions granted, boxes checked—no pacemakers or other explosives—open the retort door and shove them in. A couple hours later, I'd sweep it all out, run the bones through the grinder, pick out any hardware from the caskets and box up the ashes and label them. Twice a week I'd drive around to the area funeral homes dropping off the boxes or the urns, if they had sent an urn. No one asked about my work. Everyone wanted to be cremated, they just weren't that curious about the fire. It was perfect work for me. Simple, solitary, fixed fees and costs. I could read or tinker with the equipment. The crews would come back from their various duties—burials or mowings, setting headstones. I paid them every other week. By midafternoon I was ready for a drink. I kept a bottle of good scotch in the desk drawer.

It was Hughie MacSwiggan the insurance company sent to see me thirty years ago in the hospital, after The Fall, to offer a settlement of five thousand dollars, in trade for a promise not to sue.

"Of course, the company assumes no fault or negligence. It's only to assist in your recovery. There's hardly any cause of action here—what with the drink that had been taken." Hughie looked like Gregory Peck in *To Kill a Mockingbird*—handsome like that, but flashier, with French cuffs and a bow tie and tassel loafers.

"The doctor said it was a good thing I was drinking," I replied. "I didn't stiffen up and break my neck."

I'm not sure if I'd heard that or was making it up.

Hughie smiled, put down his briefcase, removed his hat, pulled a chair to my bedside and sat near enough to me that he could speak in the voice of a confessor or confidante.

"Listen, kid, do what you like about the money. I'm only the messenger. Here's the thing. It's a crapshoot. You can take the offer, we'll have a check in a week, you'll sign a release and that's the end of that. Or you can hire an attorney to sue for . . . pick a number . . . and the attorneys can all rattle swords at each other for the next three or four years and after your steadfast refusal not to settle for a penny less than . . . pick a number . . . the court will award you . . . pick a number . . . and your man will get half of it and two thirds of whatever is left will go for 'costs'—depositions and inquisitions, research and transcripts and such, and after all the dust clears you'll get five thousand, if the guy you've hired is worth his salt. He and our attorney will meet at the golf course to toast your perseverance. Of course, it could go the other way. You could end up with nothing, what with the party, and the underage drinking and the designer drugs, the judge might say you're lucky to be alive and let it go at that. Do what you want. It's not my money either way."

I could see why the company would send someone like Hughie. He was what my father would have called a closer—someone who made perfect sense. But then he got even closer still and began to speak in such a quiet, calming tone, I had to watch his mouth to see him shape the words to get them.

"But listen, kid, if you really believe that load of shit about how lucky you were to be drinking, how it probably saved your life; if you have really convinced yourself that being drunk when you do a backflip off of some slum landlord's third story is all to the good, you've got more problems than any amount of money will solve. And they'll likely get worse before they get better. So if it dawns on you, after you've spent the next six months in a cast, sleeping on your belly, out of school, out of work; if it ever occurs to you that you might have a problem with drink, well, that's a problem I know some things about. And maybe I can help."

He stood up, buttoned his jacket, straightened his arms so that the monogrammed French cuffs showed just below the sleeve of his jacket. He took a business card from his suit coat pocket, a pen from his shirt pocket and began writing something on the back.

"The number on the front's for talking money. You can call during regular business hours. The number on the back's my home phone. Call anytime to talk about," he paused to put the pen back in his shirt pocket, "to talk about, life. One's no good without the other. Call before you take another drink. Call before you take another dive. Next time you might not bounce."

I never called the number on the back. I took the easy money, spent it on nothing memorable, went on with my twenties and thirties unencumbered by any lasting damage from The Fall. Life just seemed to happen to me—the marriage, the twins, the business. I joined the Rotary Club and the Masons. I was president of the Chamber of Commerce. I served on the hospital board and played golf. We went to church. Every year we went camping. We bought a boat and motor home. We had a dog and then another.

I never saw Hughie again except in passing, until twenty years later when I turned up, court-ordered, to my first AA meeting after a DUI. The cop who popped me didn't know who I was. I was driving home from a card game at the Lodge. It was 2 a.m. and the streets were quiet and he pulled me over for driving without my headlights on. Hell, in the old days Chief Averill would have been playing cards with us and would have called some cars to escort us home safely. He'd hit us up later for a donation to the Police Athletic League. But this kid with his flashlight and steroid physique asks to see my driver's license, asks how much I've had to drink, asks me to step out of my car, asks me to walk along the road, then takes my keys and takes me in. I've never been so pissed off in my life.

My attorney, a fellow Rotarian, was able to keep me out of jail by mentioning my standing in the community and on my promise to get help with what the judge, a brother Mason, called my "drinking problem." I was sentenced to "ninety in ninety," meaning an Alcoholics Anonymous meeting every day for ninety days. There were weekly urine tests—the indignity of it—and my driving was restricted to AA meetings and work. Of course I wouldn't go to one of the local meetings, at St. Michael's or the Presbyterians— no need to get the chattering classes going around town. Instead, I went over to a hospital in the next township where they had a couple meetings every day, at midmorning and after dinner.

And there was Hughie, looking distinguished in his mid-sixties now, handsome as ever but more relaxed—more flannel than French cuffs, more at ease, looking like my father might have looked if he'd missed that bridge abutment years ago. When it came his turn, Hughie said his name and that he was "a grateful recovering alcoholic," and then gave anyone who'd listen—some of the inpatients there were too far gone—a brief narrative of his life and times.

How he never drank before he went to war. How he returned from the South Pacific skinny, malarial, and alcoholic, "trained by the U.S. Marine Corps for everything but living life on life's terms. I could survive the jungle, the Japs and World War II, just not marriage, peacetime, and parenthood." He married the first woman he'd had sex with, not counting the ones he'd paid for in Melbourne and China. He bought a bungalow in the suburbs and went to work selling insurance. After a son and a daughter and more trouble with drink, his first wife left him to "cut her losses." He married again, fathered again, got fired from the agency and divorced again. There followed a decade of brief incarcerations for bar fights and drunk driving, a bankruptcy filing and, after a remarkable comeback financially, what he called a moment of clarity when it occurred to him that everything he'd touched "had turned to shit."

"It was the brand-new Cadillac I drove into a telephone pole on Northwestern Highway that made me see the light. I'd been dry for a couple weeks, things were going good, I just stopped into a joint on the way home for a beer. However many hours later it was when I crashed the car, I walked away from it. I got out, like I'd just had a tire gone flat, not head-on into a goddamn telephone pole. I just got out and was walking down the street looking for a telephone booth to call the dealer and tell him to bring me another, like the whole world was my bartender, 'I'll have another,' when the thing blew up—this huge fire ball!—that's the light I saw. My 1968, red leather interior, V-8 400-some horsepower exploding light bulb—that was my moment of clarity."

He joined AA mostly because he couldn't afford a therapist. After the big agency fired him, he opened his own little insurance office and married Annette after she'd kept his fledgling business afloat for several years. They never had any children, but she kept him solvent and upright, made him take her out to dinner and dancing and mended his relations with his own daughters and son who'd grown distant in his drinking years. They had grown, in spite of his absence or because of it, into adults he loved and admired and had children of their own who thought of Hughie as a kindly "Papa." For reasons he wasn't entirely certain of he had put together "quite a few twenty-four hours of sobriety" and was grateful for the fact he "wouldn't be drinking today."

"I believe what they told me," Hughie concluded, "we alkies only have three options. Get well, go crazy, or die. If I'm not getting better, I'm getting worse. That's why I keep coming back. I don't take the first drink." He held up the thumb of his right hand for punctuation, then the index finger. "And I go to meetings. Everything else seems to fall into place."

People were nodding and smiling and wiping their eyes and fidgeting in their seats and looking at their watches and Hughie was wrapping up.

"Keep it simple," he said and thrust his thumb up in front of him again with purpose. "Don't take a drink," then lifting his index finger beside it said, "go to meetings." There was general applause and that was the end.

I did my ninety meetings, kept all my appointments with the probation department, passed my piss tests and managed to keep from taking a drink for most of the next two years, keeping in contact with Hughie, who'd become my sponsor—someone to call when things got crazy and I wanted to drink.

I might've stayed on the wagon all the way except for the pain in my ass. It would start in my lower back, work its way down my right buttock, down the right leg and into the ankle where the whole damn thing would throb away. I couldn't sit comfortably, I couldn't stand for very long, I couldn't walk around the block. It was a low-grade, ever-present, occasionally flaring pain that ran up my leg into the middle of my gluteus damn maximus and down again. I self-diagnosed as residual damage done me years ago by The Fall or maybe aggravated by lifting too much. It woke me one night with a start, out of a sound sleep, like those sudden dreams of rapid descent, the pain in my ankle flaring badly and I came downstairs and poured myself one short one, from the bottle I kept for visitors—just to take the edge off the pain of it, and to get myself back to sleep. My wife woke me up the next morning in the wingback chair, the bottle empty, the weather channel on the TV, the pain in my hindquarter still killing me. I tried the chiropractor and massage. I even tried acupuncture to no avail. I did the stretching and the hanging from the door jamb and the ice packs and the heating pads and all the rest. But nothing would soothe it like a stiff drink and some drugs.

After a couple years of on-again-off-again binge drinking and drying out and popping Oxycontin for the chronic pain, I found myself fairly dulled to everything. I managed on a kind of automatic pilot, coming and going between the house and office, joylessly, painlessly, biding time, waiting for whatever was going to happen next. The twins were away at college. My wife it seems had developed her own life into which I could come or go as I pleased, like something modular but optional. We stopped eating together. Sex was lackluster, hit-and-miss. She'd have plans most evenings— something at church or with one of her civic groups. The daily routines lost their meaning to me, becoming a slow procession of dull details. I felt no pain, my own or anyone's. It freed me up to come and go as I pleased. I spent lots of time at the Lodge and country club, long boozy lunches with the Chamber of Commerce crowd. I wrote it off to business promotion. I never would have called this happiness, or sadness. The range of my emotions had narrowed, it seemed. The best I could manage was an absence of pain. I didn't want to chance tampering with that.

For a while, Hughie tried to get me to quit. He'd call me and offer to come get me and take me to a meeting. I'd give him one or another excuse. After a while he quit calling too. Every so often he'd send a card that read "How go the wars, kid?" or "Had enough?" and always included a number to call, "day or night, 24/7 whenever you're ready." After a while he quit sending cards.

And I stayed at the office more. The area was growing. Farms turning into golf courses and subdivisions, we had a respectable traffic jam through town in the morning, the Chamber of Commerce membership was booming, funeral homes doing land office business, people dropping like flies. I was running the retorts day and night. First it was just the Episcopalians and Unitarians who cremated their dead. Over time even the Catholics did it. What had been the exception was becoming the rule. I sold the landscape equipment to one of the Mexicans who took over the grave digging and cemetery maintenance. It was all I could do to keep up with the cremations. Along one wall of the pole barn bodies in caskets and cardboard boxes were lining up, waiting their turn in one of the chambers. I walled off one end of the pole barn and put in a shower and toilet and bed. Nobody seemed to miss me at home. The twins were off living their lives. My wife seemed happy enough on her own. I put in cable TV, a sink and fridge, then a table for magazines and some shelves for books. First it was only a couple nights a week. After a while the exception became the rule and I only went home for emergencies. Otherwise I more or less lived at the crematory. I'd spend the days reading novels or newspapers, running the retorts and sorting the paperwork. I'd try not to drink before four or five, after I'd been into town for a meal. I slept in fits and starts. I kept the retorts running. Some nights between the drink that it took to be free of pain and the drink that it took to be entirely numb, when the color of the whiskey in the glass and the tinkling of the ice cubes in the glass still meant something to me, I'd stand out in the pole barn between the retorts and the waiting boxes full of patient corpses and read them poems from a book I bought at the library sale called *The New Modern American & British Poetry*. I'd paid a quarter for it.

> I'm nobody! Who are you?
> Are you nobody, too?
> Then there's a pair of us—don't tell!
> They'd banish us, you know.

I'd have to shout a little to hear myself over the roar of the retorts in the open room, echoing off of the cement floor and metal walls and ceiling.

How dreary to be somebody!
How public, like a frog.
To tell your name the livelong day
To an admiring bog![2]

The particulars of Emily Dickenson's life, detailed by the
anthologist, were a comfort to me. How she wrote in private, in secrecy, and a book of hers was never published in
her lifetime but after death she became famous. "Keeping
herself strictly to herself, she became a mystery, a legend
even in her own lifetime."
    I'd read them Frost and Rudyard Kipling and memorized
that little "Envoy" by Ernest Dowson:

They are not long, the weeping and the laughter,
Love and desire and hate;
I think they have no portion in us after
    We pass the gate.

They are not long, the days of wine and roses:
Out of a misty dream
Our path emerges for a while, then closes
    Within a dream.[3]

That always made me thirsty. I liked the rhymes. And
I'd fill my tumbler with ice and scotch and slump in the
wingback chair by my bed rummaging through the book for
further verses, muttering odds and ends of Yeats about "the
glowing bars" or "the seed of the fire flicker and glow." Or
of Edwin Arlington Robinson who named his poems after
people who seemed like people I might know, or Hilda Doolittle whose "Lethe" I could never quite memorize. Except
for the final stanza:

Nor word nor touch nor sight
Of lover, you

Shall long through the night but for this:
The roll of the full tide to cover you
Without question,
Without kiss.[4]

When the poetry didn't do it, I'd read them fiction—bits of
Moby Dick or Hemingway or this passage from "A Painful
Case," a story of Joyce's I'd read back in school that always
took my breath away:

> He lived at a little distance from his body, regarding his
> own acts with doubtful side-glances. He had an odd autobi-
> ographical habit which led him to compose in his mind from
> time to time a short sentence about himself containing a
> subject in the third person and a predicate in the past tense.[5]

Or I'd play the guitar, bought at a rummage sale, the
three or four chords I knew, bits and pieces of old folk tunes,
imagining my voice made distinctive by years of one-night
stands and hard travel. Eventually I'd pass out.

It was on such a night that Hughie called. I woke with a
start, the book hitting the floor with a flop and him standing
in front of me like an apparition. He was thinner, paler, but
handsome still, his tweed coat bagging on his shoulders, his
flannel shirt buttoned at the collar.

"Your wife said I'd find you here."

"Yes, yes, busy . . . round the clock . . ."

"How do you sleep with those furnaces going?"

He was shouting a little to be heard.

"I must be used to it. Can't hear a thing."

I wondered how long I'd been out for, what time it was. I
was thirsty but with Hughie there I couldn't drink. I offered
to make some coffee. He was looking around.

"So here's where we all go up in smoke."

"Yeah, ashes to ashes, dust to dust."

I was trying to sound in better fettle than I was.

"I've told Annette to just cremate me."

He was looking through the open door, out across the pole barn to where the retorts where running.

"Well don't be in a hurry, Hughie, we don't give any discounts till you make the hundred."

"Well I am in a hurry, kid. That's why I'm here."

The particulars of Hughie's cancer were unremarkable. He said them without drama or the precision of detail that people with diseases often are given to and finished with the best guess his doctors had given him.

"Six weeks? Six months? It's hard to know. But I've told Annette to just cremate me."

The operative word in his directive was "just." He just didn't want to trouble them further. He just wanted it all to be over—the second guessing, the treatments they kept proffering, but never a cure. He just wanted it all behind him.

"You know, I should have died in the Russell Islands. God knows some better men than me died there."

I told him I'd take care of everything, rest assured, he needn't worry. I was not comfortable with all of this. I was very thirsty. I wanted him to leave. I preferred the anonymous dead in their boxes lined up on the wall of the pole barn waiting their turn, to the living, breathing, by all accounts dying man I knew some things about, standing before me. I wanted him out of there and to be left alone.

"Easy for you to say—'don't worry'—I'll be the one with my nose pressed up against whatever is out there, or isn't. Don't bullshit a bullshitter, kid."

He sat down in the folding chair I kept by the small table that was the only other furniture in the room.

I asked him about his time in the service. Anything to change the subject.

"Never mind the Marines," he said, "no taps or flags or bugle, no eulogists or limousines, none of that. I'm not paying for a party I can't be at. I just want to be burned up before I start to smell bad; and one more thing."

He pulled his chair closer, leaned in with his elbows on his knees, his hands hanging open with uplifted palms and fixed me with his slightly jaundiced eyes.

"I want you to scatter my ashes for me. Will you promise me that, kid? You've got to take care of that part yourself. I don't want Annette and the kids. . . . Promise me."

I told him I thought his family might appreciate some place to go and pay their respects on the holidays and birthdays and anniversaries out there in the future after he died. I suggested one of the local cemeteries where three boxes of ashes could be put in a single grave.

"That's just it, kid. I don't want them anchored to me or some place where I'm buried. They can just keep me in their hearts. That's why I want to be burned and scattered. I want to travel light. Like I'm always saying, kid, 'Let go, let God.'"

I could see he wasn't budging on this. No grave or niches in Hughie's future. No together forever cut in stone.

"And where do you want the ashes scattered?" I asked as if we were talking about something other than him, as if "the ashes" might be easier; figuring maybe some hole on the golf course or in the river or lake, or possibly in the woods out behind his house. It seemed he hadn't considered this part. He was looking off into the middle distance, his eyes narrowing, deep in his contemplations, a wince or a grin—I couldn't be sure—beginning to form on his face.

"Scotland," he said quite matter-of-factly. "Yes, Scotland, that's just the place."

"Have you family there?"

"None that I know of."

I asked when he was last there and he told me he had never been. He'd always wanted to go, since way back in his drinking days when he used to be known as "Friggin MacSwiggan" in the bars. But after getting sober he would never chance it, what with all of those lovely single malts and local whiskys.

"And Annette doesn't fly," and business was either too good or too bad to take the time away and go. But now that he thought of it, now that he'd be dead before long, he'd really like to go and wasn't I just the man to take him.

"Scotland, kid, that's just the place—take me to Scotland and toss me to the wind. What's that they say? 'I'm worth it'? Well I *am* worth it, after all. So promise me you'll take me there. Or else I'll haunt you, promise."

"But I've never been out of the country," I protested. Except for a cremationists' convention once, in Albuquerque, I'd never even been on a plane.

"All the more reason. Live a little kid, get out of your comfort zone and see the world. Promise me." He was suddenly serious. "Promise me you'll get me there."

Hughie pulled out an envelope full of hundred dollar bills wrapped in thousand dollar packets and quickly counted out five of them. Of course, I objected and of course, he insisted.

"That should cover things. I'll pay the freight, kid. After that you're on your own."

He said nothing about how I'd gone missing from AA. He never asked about my drinking or the prescription drugs. So when he gathered himself up to go, I told him I hoped it would all go well for him, that he wouldn't be in any pain, and that I really wanted to thank him for all his care and kindness over the years and that maybe someday I'd get sober yet.

"It takes what it takes, kid. We all have our bottom. Who's to know? For years I thought it meant giving something up. It wasn't until later I saw it was a gift, sobriety, something I could give myself. All I had to do was ask for a little help from my friends."

I nodded and smiled.

"I'm an alkie who's not dying of alcoholism. That's miracle enough for me, kid. The rest is gravy."

I nodded some more and shook his hand.

"Do you think if they told me when they showed me this

cancer, 'so Hughie, just don't eat cabbage and go to these meetings and this cancer, this squamous cell metastasized carcinoma, will never kill you'—do you think I'd have any trouble with quitting cabbage or doing the meetings? Not on your life, kid. Well, not on mine."

When Hughie died Annette kept him at home, put on some Tommy Dorsey and Glenn Miller music and called some of the AA crowd and they announced it at the local meetings and all that evening and the next they kept Hughie there while folks came by to pay their respects and tell Annette and the kids exactly how much Hughie had meant to them. An AA friend who worked for a funeral home fixed him up a little, closed his eyes and mouth, filed the paperwork and brought a box.

The next morning, his daughters and son lifted his body into the box, into the hearse and they and Annette all followed behind while the handful of friends and neighbors sang the Marine Corps hymn while the little procession drove Hughie down the driveway and out of sight. I went ahead to meet them at my place. I had the retort fired up, preheated and at the ready. I rolled Hughie on to a hydraulic lift, put the little numbered metal coin on the box to keep track of Hughie after the burning, and pushed the box into the retort, closed the door and pressed the red button that filled the chamber with fire that burned his body and the box. Annette wiped her eyes, thanked me for everything and handed me an envelope. When I insisted that Hughie had paid for everything she said that I was not to open it until I was on the plane on the way to Scotland. "I'm just following instructions," she told me, then hugged me and went away.

After everything had cooled, I ground his larger bone structures into a finer substance and dumped all of it in a plastic bag inside a plastic box with a label that bore his names and dates and the logo of the crematory. This greatly reduced version of Hughie was kept on the table in my room till I could arrange for a passport and get my ticket sorted and pack my bags and say my goodbyes and get through the long list of procrastinations that had kept me from going anywhere before. Days went to weeks which went to months. For the first few nights he was there on my table, I'd pour myself a tall one, cobble some elegiac blather together, hoist the tumbler saying, "Here's to ya, Hughie!" recite some poems and get a little tipsy with him. But more and more I began to feel stupid, talking to a box of ashes, especially one that had managed, in his own time, to keep sober. I drank less, then little, then none at all. "You've ruined it for me," I whispered to the ashes, one night when the whiskey wouldn't do it. And one night after that, I opened the box, undid the twist tie to the plastic bag, and poured the last bit of a near empty bottle of pricey scotch over Hughie and said, "Have one on me, pal." The poems I kept reading to the box sounded suddenly new to me. I slept well after that. I bought a ticket to Scotland the following day.

I taught one of the Mexicans to run the retort. He said he'd take care of things while I was gone.

When the x-ray at the airport showed "some dense packaging" in my carry-on, I told the security guard it was Hughie MacSwiggan's cremated remains and asked if she'd like to inspect them further. She looked a little panicked, shook her head, and let me pass. Somewhere over the Atlantic I opened the envelope Annette had given me. Inside was a list of AA meetings in Edinburgh—dozens of them, every day all over town, written out in Hughie's scribble. There was a detailed street map with the locations marked in red ink. And a note from Hughie in the same red ink that read, "Have one on me, kid," paper clipped to a Bank of Scotland one pound note.

I did not declare Hughie at customs in Heathrow and kept to my own counsel on the train ride north and said nothing checking in at the Channings Hotel. I considered the gardens off Princes Street or maybe some corner of the castle grounds, but the festival goers made those impossible—the swarm of them everywhere, everywhere. I toyed with the notion of leaving him in a public house near Waverley Station on the theory that heaven for Hughie might mean that he could drink again. Maybe a fellow pilgrim would find him there and put him to some providential use. But it was the view from Dean Bridge, the deep valley, the "dene" that names the place, the river working its way below under the generous overhang of trees, the scale of it all and the privacy. I worked my way down into Belgrave Crescent where I found an open, unlocked gate to the private gardens there. But it was a little too perfect, a little too rose-gardeny and manicured and I was drawn by the sound of falling water.

So I went out and around past the Dean Parish Church, and the graveyard there. I made my way down to the water by the footpath, and working back in the direction of the bridge, I found a small waterfall, apparently the site of an old mill, and poured Hughie's ashes out—some into the curling top waters and the rest into the circling pool below. I knelt to the duty of it and watched till every bit of him was gone.

Chapter Sixteen

Movable and Steadfast Feasts

M y old dog Bill will be dead by Easter. God knows, he should have been dead before now. The now of which I write—the moment to hand—is that no man's land of days between Christmas, New Year's, and the Epiphany. I've gone beyond fashionably late with this essay which I promised for the twelfth day of the twelfth month of the last year—an essay on Easter with an Advent delivery. I've promised it now for little Christmas, hoping that like the magi of old, I'll come to see things as they are.

A member of the reverend clergy told me that the formula old preachers used to prepare their homiletics included three points and a poem. Montaigne would string his essays on a filigree of Latin poets. He worked in his library and when stuck for some leap into a fresh paragraph, he'd often quote Virgil or Catullus or Lucan and carry on as if the poem were an aperitif readying the reader for another course.

Which puts me in mind of the twelve days of Christmas I spent downstate being paterfamilias for our yuletide observations. This poem came into being in contemplation of a carol we always sing this time of year.

TWELVE DAYS OF CHRISTMAS

Some pilgrims claim the carol is a code
for true believers and their catechists,
to wit: four colly birds, four gospel texts,
eight maids a milking, the beatitudes,
and pipers piping, the eleven left
once Judas had betrayed the lamb of God—
that partridge in a pear tree, the holy one
and only whose nativity becomes
in just a dozen days the starlit eve
of three French hens with their epiphanies
huddled round the family in the manger,
tendering their gold and frankincense and myrrh.
The whole tune seems to turn on "five gold rings"—
the Pentateuch, those first books of the Torah
in which ten lords a leaping stand in for
the ten commandments cut in loaves of stone
which Moses broke over his wayward tribesmen.
Two turtle doves, two testaments, old and new.
Six geese a laying, creation's shortened week,
the swimming swans, gifts of the Holy Ghost
whose fruits become withal nine ladies dancing.
Twelve drummers drumming, the Apostles' Creed:
a dozen doctrines to profess belief in.
Still, others say it's only meant to praise
fine feathered birds and characters and rings,
our singing nothing more than thanksgiving
for litanies of undeserved grace,
unnumbered blessings, the light's increasing,
our brightly festooned trees bedazzling.[1]

Montaigne, the father of all essayists, himself a sort of preacher, to four centuries of readers and counting, was anxious to understand the human being and condition. It was, thanks be, his lifelong study. In his marvelous essay, "Of

Repentance," a Lenten read and Easter anthem, he wrote in French a point that "Englishes," "In every man is the whole of man's estate," by which he meant we are all at once the same but different; to know the species, know a specimen. To understand the Risen Christ, we'd better reckon with the wounds and miracles, betrayals and agonies. Study the Scriptures and the poems.

The men in my Bible study took the day off after Christmas last week, but we met for the day after New Year's today, in the early morning dark at the funeral home, as we have been doing now for years. The price is right, the coffee's free; it's quiet in the early o'clock. Except for the ones gone to their time shares in Florida, or the ones homebound with the seasonable woo, the turnout is a good one and we're glad to have survived into another year. We read from the twenty-fourth chapter of Matthew when Jesus is giving the disciples a list of the signs that the end times are nearing. Wars and rumors of wars, false prophets, nation rising up against nation, earthquakes and famines in various places.

The sky has been falling through most of history. And for everyone predicting doom, the doom is certain. Whether we die en masse, in cataclysms of natural or supernatural origin, we die in fact, 100 percent.

Possibly this is why one of us eases the talk around to declaring a win in the "War on Christmas," reporting that people are saying "Merry Christmas" now in a way that political correctness prevented up until now. Another fellow heartily agrees. I mention that the War on Christmas was invented by a cable news host to divert attention from the wars in Afghanistan and Iraq, which were coming, alas too late, under scrutiny in the middle noughties. I suggest they go home and Google "Barack Obama and Merry Christmas." And I wondered aloud, it being the feast of the Octave of Christmas, which used to observe in the Christian calendar the circumcision of Jesus, why these old, white, male, and much-aggrieved Christians weren't willing to serve in the "War on Circumcision." Why should we wish each other "Happy New Year" when "Happy Circumcision" is the more Christian, more religious greeting? They tilted their heads at what I was saying the way that Bill does when he hears an oddly pitched noise. But I digress; I was trying to relate Easter to Bill's slow demise. This is not about birth and circumcision and magi, rather betrayal, passion, death, and burial, and then the Easter we claim to believe in.

He's lived well past the expectations—Bill, the dog—half again beyond his "use by" date. These latter days have all been bonus time and have taught me gratitude in the stead of the "poor me's" and the "why me's" and the "give me's," which have always seemed my usual nature. I'm easily beset by resentments and begrudgeries—a character flaw from which I've achieved irregular remissions over the years, occasional dispensations. I'm living through one such dispensation now, watching old Bill in his withering and bewilderments as the mightiness of his shoulders and hindquarters, the deep menace of his guardian bark, and the fathomless pools of his big brown eyes have given way to lame waltzing on his "last legs," a kind of castrato's cough at threats he senses but cannot see through a cloud of cataracts, nor hear in the dull chambers of lost itching ears. His nose still works its cold damp magic. He finds his food and good places to squat to the duties of his toilet. His soft black curls of fur are full of dander and dry skin beneath, despite a designer mash of essential oils and my wife's tender correctives. So long as he eats and craps and can be medicated against the pain, I willn't exercise the lethal dominion over him I wish I did not have. Yes, dead by Easter I'd wager, or sooner, much sooner, as the gyre of demise works its tightening, ineluctable damage.

Back when I was researching his breed, the Bernese Mountain dog, or as I joked when he was a puppy, "an AKC-registered Pain in the Ass," the Wikipedia on my old laptop promised six to eight years of life expectancy for dogs of his prodigious size. All to the good, I remember thinking, at least I'll outlive him so. I was fifty-seven years old that late winter I got him, now twelve years ago. I was well into my last trimester of being. My father, my grandfathers, the men in my line had all died in their sixties, of broken hearts: a bad valve, clogged arteries, congestive heart failure, some embolism—quick, convincing "failures," or "attacks," or "infarctions."

Bill's gone half again older than we expected. And even that might have been a miscalculation. My wife never really wanted a dog. After the kids were grown and gone and out on their own on automatic pilot, throwing in with partners of the same species, taking mortgages, signing leases, making plans and car payments, after we breathed the sigh of relief that they all seemed poised and provisioned to outlive us, Mary settled in with *Law and Order* reruns and I kept to my old customs of splitting my time between the day job undertaking and the preoccupation with language, writing, and words.

I remember sitting with her one Sunday afternoon, watching the episode where Lennie and his estranged daughter, Cathy, meet up for lunch—she keeps her distance because of his drinking, and the two failed marriages, one to her mother. The episode, "Aftershock," involves Lennie and Rey Curtis, his young partner, along with Jack McCoy and Claire Kincaid, the legal team, witnessing an execution of someone they put away. Lennie's life was always complex. And I was thinking what a good thing a dog would be to get me out of the house and walking on a regular basis and I said, on one of the commercial breaks, "What would you think about my getting a dog?"

"Are you out of your (expletive deleted) mind?" she responded. "Finally we have the place to ourselves, we come and go as we please, we've got some peace and quiet, and you want a dog!" I took this to mean she didn't want one.

In those days I would occasionally write a poem that borrowed from a famous poem for the kernel of creation that brought it into being. This is how I'd come to write a poem called, "Corpses Do Not Fret Their Coffin Boards," which borrowed unabashedly from William Wordsworth's sonnet, "Nuns Fret Not at Their Convent's Narrow Room," which I'd encountered that morning, possibly on the radio, listening to the voice of Garrison Keillor who used to do "The Writers' Almanac," a five-minute diamond of daily bits and pieces that ended with the reading of a poem. Wordsworth's sonnet is in praise of sonnets, in observation of the truth revealed to him, some centuries back, that formal constraints—"the narrow rooms"—often produce an unpredictable freedom. The sonneteer knows all too well the work in words to make a sonnet is but fourteen lines of ten or so syllables, organized to rhyme in some predetermined way—a code which poets map out as AABB or ABAB, or maybe, as Wordsworth did for his wee sonnet, ABBA, with the twist that the sound of A in lines one and four, repeats itself in lines five and eight. There are other embellishments of sound and sense to bring it to an end in line fourteen, but what I can say is that one comes to the close of a sonnet with a sense that it must have been a loving God that brought old Wordsworth into being to speak to me years after his demise in a different century, millennium, and nation.

Wordsworth affirms the snug hugging and liberation of the sonnet's terms in the last half of his, to wit:

> In truth the prison, into which we doom
> Ourselves, no prison is: and hence for me,
> In sundry moods, 'twas pastime to be bound
> Within the Sonnet's scanty plot of ground;
> Pleased if some Souls (for such there needs must be)
> Who have felt the weight of too much liberty,
> Should find brief solace there, as I have found.[2]

My own sonnet, while crediting Wordsworth, albeit sub-
titularly, has less to do with space and nature than with time
and money, preoccupations of my advancing years.

CORPSES DO NOT FRET THEIR COFFIN BOARDS
after Wordsworth

Corpses do not fret their coffin boards,
nor bodies wound in love their narrow beds:
size matters less to lovers and the dead
than to the lonely and the self-absorbed
for whom each passing moment is a chore
and space but vacancy: unholy dread
of what might happen or not happen next;
this dull predicament of less or more's
a never balanced book, whereas for me,
the worth of words is something I can count
out easily, on fingertips—the sounds
they make, the sense, their coins and currencies —
these denouements doled out in tens, fourteens:
last reckonings tapped out on all accounts.[3]

Fresh from its typing, this is the page I posted to the
fridge with a kitchen magnet back in the day before stainless
steel appliances made magnets redundant, the better for my
missus to see it in her own good time and possibly ink some
edits in as marginalia. I loved it when she read my poems
and commented for better or worse because it sang to me a
song of hope beyond the everyday desolation of long con-
sortium, often marked by romantic indifference and connu-
bial blahs in the stead of bliss.

But days after I'd posted the draft, alas, no corrections or
comments had appeared. No cross-outs or smiley faces, no
affirmations scribbled in passing, no nothing.

It was another Sunday afternoon when, being as I am a man of habits, I said into the general silence of the day that was in it, "What would you think about my getting a dog?" To which she replied without enthusiasm, "Maybe you could name it 'Wordsworth.'"

My heart leaped inside my bosom. I couldn't believe my ears. What meaning ought I take from this expletive-free and contingent utterance? Surely, it seemed, she had read my poem, or at least the title and citation line. Was this some signal of approval, some sign that my efforts had not been for naught? At the very least it was not disapproval, no rhetorical about the state of my (formerly expletive-ridden) mind. No, this was, if not full-throated approval, a willingness to consider the prospect, a nod toward tolerance if not the full embrace of the notion. I moved, immediately, into my office, where my computer, ever at the ready, soon had me Googling for "Bernese Mountain Dogs, Michigan." Two days later I was driving up the highway with my middle son, to mid Michigan, where a man claimed to be weaning a recent litter.

"What about 'No!' didn't you understand?" she said, when I brought the puppy in the door. "But honey," I coaxed her, "we can call him Wordsworth! Just like you said. William Wordsworth."

"Let's just make it 'Bill W.,'" she said insinuating the name of the founder of the fellowship of Alcoholics Anonymous, a fellowship to which we both belonged. Was she insinuating that the puppy might shake the serenity that our long sobriety had produced?

It is hard to know, but "Bill" it has been ever since—from the eleven-pound puppy he was that Ash Wednesday of 2006, that first of March I brought him through the door on the day of my only daughter's birthday, to the hundred-and-ten-pound giant of kindliness he in time became, to the withering, arthritic, ninety-some-pound geriatric pooch snoring on the floor next to my shoes as I type these truths into the computer.

In the twelve years since, so much has happened. If I take stock, it is an inventory of losses. My daughter, now in her middle years, has disconnected from her family. She is estranged from her mother, my first wife, and from me, her stepmother, her brothers and her brothers' families, her aunts and uncles and cousins, everyone from her family of origin. In the email asking us to keep our distance and not to initiate any contact with her, she said she was going out West for therapy to treat what she called her codependence. She said that she felt that she never got enough time as a child, that she had to grow up too soon, what with the divorce between her mother and me when she was nine and ten years old. I wrote back saying that such insights were hard got and that I supported her eagerness to get right with herself and would follow her directives and stood ready to assist in any way I might do her some good in her efforts. Except for the occasional text message, to wish happy birthdays or best for holidays, we've had no substantial communication since. Her family of choice, near as I can figure, includes her husband, her horse, her dog, some friends?

Before this happened, I spent two years in weekly therapy with her in an effort to discern what might be done to let this cup pass. The shrink thought we'd arrived at a plan for what to do to keep us in each other's futures. But soon after that, my daughter wrote to say her well-being required that she keep her distance from us all. I said I wanted her to be well. It feels like a death without any of the comforting, buffering infrastructure of mortality—a known cause and certification, ceremony, a grave, a place I can go and weep. There's none of that. Her absence, her choice of absence, her riddance of us all is everywhere. On holidays and birthdays there's a text that comes more or less as a proof of life. For years it seemed I was left with a choice between assigning this sadness to evil or mental illness. I chose the latter. There is no succor in it.

Whether this grief is coincident with, correlated to, or the cause of our lackluster marriage—the second one, or maybe the first—I do not know. But what I do know is we've lost our way. We live, for the most part, separate lives and have slowly ceased to share our lives, our dreams, our meals, our bed, our whereabouts, our hopes and fears, our plans for the future. The desolation is as palpable as our bliss once seemed. All of this after many years of joyous intimacy, shared purpose, real partnership makes it more the pity that we both live now like widowed people, bereft of a spouse that, though still alive, is gone from us in measurable ways. We share bank accounts and an estate plan and rise to the occasion for holidays, but otherwise are in every meaningful way alone, and what has grown between us is what Heaney called a "silence beyond silence listened for." It seems I've ended up like Lennie Briscoe—a two-time loser at marriage, estranged from a daughter who chooses to remain out of contact with or from her family of origin. We text our affections or proclaim them to anyone in earshot but it makes no difference. When I compare my lot to men I've buried, whose flaws and imperfections seemed amplified compared to mine, and yet whose wives still went along for the ride, whose daughters doted on them till the end, like a hurt dog howling at the emptiness, I shake a fist in the face of the God I don't quite believe in anymore.

The poor me and why me lamentations, variations on the book of Job, leave me with a choice between hurt and anger. I tend toward the latter and fear the worst. I keep working the program, the fellowship, and twelve steps of AA, because it keeps me from adding a class A depressant to the gathering sadness, the tears of things. I do not want to live in fear.

My pal, George, is what we call a "sponsor"—someone in the fellowship to reach out to when the ways of things threaten to overwhelm. He's been sober longer than anyone I know. And he's bookish and very well educated: he's a JD and CPA, and for a good few of my books, was the proofreader I sent the roughest of drafts to. He'd fix the

spelling and punctuation and errors of thought and construction. We've been friends and neighbors for decades
now. For years he's been losing his short-term memory. The
arc of his infirmity has been slow but steady. Dithering gave
way to a sort of discombobulation, which in time gave way
to chronic disorientation, which became what seems now
a cruel advancing dementia. Beyond the indignities of age,
his condition rightly frightened his family. They got him
into assisted living. Attendant nurses see to his meds and
meals. There are bingo nights and socials. I call and visit
when I can. I live upstate now, three weeks out of four, at
a lake house with Bill for whom the remove and the quiet
are like balms. He doesn't have young suburbanites to bark
at out the windows as they stroll by with their toddlers,
infants, and designer dogs. Downstate, my wife occupies the
house next to the funeral home where I lived for forty-five
years and into which she moved, when my sons and daughters were school children or teenagers and I was the family
court's designee as the "more fit" custodial parent—all of us
hobbled some by the end of the marriage that brought them
into being.

I call George a couple times a week to see how he's doing.
When I asked him how he was adjusting to living there he
told me what I guess I needed to hear. "I'm doing fine," he
said, "you can't be angry all the time." It makes me believe
in a loving God when deep in my resentments about living
alone I hear my sponsor, though addled and beset, bewildered really and yet making perfect sense to me. Good to
have just such a sponsor. You can tell him anything and he'll
likely forget. Sometimes I think it might be a gift except
when I see the thousand-yard stare he sometimes gets, like
combat soldiers who have seen too much, or keep getting a
glimpse of what they can't remember anymore. I took him
to the movies a couple months ago. We saw *Dunkirk*, ate
popcorn and Milk Duds. It was fun. On the way out of the
theater he quoted some lines from Churchill's speech to

Parliament regarding Dunkirk, "*We shall* defend our island, whatever the cost may be, *we shall fight on the beaches, we shall fight* on the landing grounds, *we shall fight* in the fields and in the streets, *we shall fight* in the hills; *we shall* never surrender"; something he'd remembered from his lifelong studies and erudition. By the time I dropped him back to his quarters in the care facility, he could not remember what movie we'd seen.

Surrender's a big part of staying sober. "Let go," we alkies often say, "let God." LG, LG! Or, "not our day to watch it," meaning we are not in charge. It's why I address my supplications to Whomever's in Charge Here, because the article of faith I hold to is provisional, to wit, if there's a God, it isn't me. The fellowship has ruined my religious certainty— that One True Faith-ism we all are raised with. But the fellowship of wounded, variously damaged goods who've shared their experience, strength, and hopes with me have illumined for me, however dimly, a life of faith. It's made me wary of certainty and open to hopes and loves I never before imagined. It's made me grateful and rheumy eyed so that I find myself weeping at the ways of things, *De Rerum Natura* Lucretius called it—the glimpses of godliness we sometimes get in the otherwise quotidian, dull happenstance of life. Lucretius was a disbeliever, whereas I'm a happy ignoramus. In either case, we do not know.

The things George still remembers best are often things that happened years ago, like the woman who told him at his mother's funeral how his mother "understood life's higher callings." He remembers that as the high praise it was of a woman who took to heart the hardships of others and did what she could to make their situations better. I tell him I think he has that too, an understanding of life's higher callings, how he's been a source for me of good orderly direction, if not the voice of God, at least a goodness in him that is undeniable. He looks out the window at the birds in the snow—chickadees and nuthatches, titmice and a cardinal—and asks if I believe it means an angel is near, to see a bright red cardinal in the chill of winter. Perhaps, I tell him, it's his mother, or mine. He looks away; I'm getting rheumy eyed.

I had Bill's grave dug two years ago, fearful as I was of getting caught by frost deep in the ground, with a dead dog on my hands in Michigan's winter. And I started collecting the soup bones, littered everywhere over the yard, which he had worked the marrow out of over the years. It got to where I'd have them custom cut at the butchers, a few dozen at a time. I found a couple hundred of them and strung them on a line of rope and wound some solar-powered lights around the rope and hung the whole assemblage from the fulcrum that overhangs the water's edge and by which the former tenants' dock was swung out into place each spring. The bone rosary is what I call it, this blinking string of bones and lights that's meant to mark the spot where Bill will be interred sometime in the coming spring, I reckon, when his age and infirmity come to the certain end all living things come to. I've even written a brief lament and asked my son to have it cast in bronze so I can bolt it to a stone over his grave.

LITTLE ELEGY
for a dog who skipped out, and after XJ Kennedy

Here lies loyal, trusted, true
friend for life, Bill W.,
named for Wordsworth and the guy
by whose twelve steps I've stayed dry,

sober even, these long years,
like the good dog buried here
who could bark but never bit;
never strayed too far or shit

indoors; never fell from grace.
God, grant him this ground, this grave,
out of harms' way, ceaseless rest.
Of all good dogs old Bill was best.

They laugh at me, of course, my sons, for all the planning for Bill's demise—the hole at the corner of the lot, the rosary of bones blinking in the dark over the water's edge, the stone, the little poem. Preparing for Bill's death, they figure, is a way of preparing for my own or diverting my attention from fears about what lies ahead, in the way that Easter has, for true believers, been a blessed assurance of eternal life; a contingent balm, in its alternate narrative, in the gaping maw of mortality.

I've a friend who says we've lost our "eschatological nerve," the certainty that heaven awaits the good and perdition, the evildoers. With the loss of a sense of eternal reward or damnation producing justice in a world so often unfair, we've begun to uphold the so-called prosperity gospel, to wit, success is a sign of God's favor, as if grace was deserved or earned like the poverty the poor are said to have coming to them. The good news formerly proclaimed by the evangels has been replaced by their enthusiasm for Donald Trump and his zero-sum, winners-and-losers agenda.

This year Easter falls on April Fools'. Some feasts are movable, some steadfast. It'll also be, if my friend George remains, as he has since April 1, 1974, quit of the booze that made him crazy, his forty-fourth AA birthday, proving, as he often says, that any fool can get sober if he or she works the program. Whether March Madness or April Fools', Easter is for those who believe in second acts and second chances, another go, mulligans and do overs. Easter is for repentance and forgiveness, amends and abundant life. Easter is when the lost are found and the dead arise, transfigured, glorified by what is possible. The Easter I believed in as a boy was a sort of zombie apocalypse. It never mattered much to me whether Jesus was really raised from the dead. Like Lennie Briscoe, I was damaged at the specter of the capital punishment. The broken, bloody body of the Christ that hung center stage in Catholic churches was more a spectacle to me than narrative. Perhaps that's sacrilege. Maybe not. Nor have I much interest in whether the moral influence or substitutionary atonement models of redemption most apply. My faith in a loving God, keeping a count of the hairs on my head, comes and goes with changing realities. It is as if I blame every outrage, every evil not averted, every sadness that might have been undone, on the God I hardly believe in anymore. Some days I see the hand or hear the voice of God implicated in the things that happen; others not so much. Begrudgery and resentment are the crosses I bear and I find them much heavier than just giving thanks. This Easter I'm not looking for an empty tomb, triumphant savior, or life eternal. Rather, some spiritual progress, instead of perfection; a little repair if not redemption, some salvage south of full salvation. "No appointments," an old timer used to tell me, "no disappointments." No expectations, no vexations.

Truth told I see sufficient triumph in the way that Bill still makes the climb upstairs at night, despite his sore hips, cloudy eyes, and the withered muscle mass in his shoulders and hindquarters. It comes with age. Is he driven by loyalty or an old fear of sleeping alone? Is it love or fear of loss? Impossible to know. He carries on but does not speak.

I see an Easter in George's getting through another day of his assisted but nonetheless bewildered living, in good humor though utterly out of sorts. I sense it in the texts I get from my long-estranged daughter, those proofs of life; the flickering of tenderness I still feel toward my distant wife, our genial courtesies.

The meeting I go to on Sunday nights up at the lake is in the basement of Transfiguration Church. And that's what I'm after this Easter, I think. That's what I'm after most of the time, the momentary radiance of the divine beaming out of God's creation. Old dogs can do it, old friends, old wives; old sorrows borne patiently, old grievances forgiven, old connections restored.

New ones too, like the other night at the meeting when Lilah was talking. She's the youngest pilgrim at the table. She's paid her dues and is working on sobriety. She's talking about how she came to know that she was beloved, when her girlfriend, noticing how badly sunburned Lilah got when they were gardening one August afternoon last summer, did not scold. Rather, she carefully peeled the dry shreds of skin off of Lilah's reddened shoulder, bent and tenderly kissed the spot, and held the desiccated remnants of her darling's flesh in the palm of her hand, like viaticum, a sort of holy grail which she brought to her mouth, ate, and swallowed.

Her sharing this intimacy and its intelligence quickened my breath and then caught it up. Gobsmacked is what I was, my mouth agape as if trying to hold my breath and let it go. My eyes were getting red and rheumy yet again, welling with a glimpse of the divine, the beautiful, the redeemed and atoned for, manifestly forgiven beings, all of us assembled round the table, we had shown up broken and bewildered and disconnected and were suddenly beatified, illumined, and made new, transfigured in the shimmering moment; my catching breaths were shortening and I was fearless suddenly, cavalier about the scene I was on the brink of making.

It was then I was remembering that Jesus wept.

Permissions

Notes

Chapter 1: Every Cradle Asks Us "Whence?"

1. Billy Collins, "Aristotle," in *Picnic, Lightning* (Pittsburgh: University of Pittsburgh Press, 1998), 100.
2. Robert G. Ingersoll, "At a Child's Grave," in *The Best of Robert Ingersoll*, ed. Roger E. Greeley (Amherst, NY: Prometheus Books, 1993), 111–12.
3. Thomas G. Long, *Accompany Them with Singing—The Christian Funeral* (Louisville, KY: Westminster John Knox Press, 2009), 73.

Chapter 2: And Every Coffin, "Whither?"

1. Collins, "Aristotle," 100–101.
2. Ibid., 101.
3. Oscar Hijuelos, *Mr. Ives' Christmas* (New York: HarperCollins, 1995), 100–101.
4. Albert Annett and Alice E. Lehtinen, "Laban Ainsworth," JaffreyHistory.org, http://www.jaffreyhistory.org/05people /biographies/ainsworth_laban/ainsworth_laban.php.
5. Thomas Lynch, "Oh Say Grim Death," in *Walking Papers: Poems* (New York: W. W. Norton, 2010), 25–26.
6. Tennessee Williams, *The Glass Menagerie* (New York: New Directions, 1999), 4–5.

7. Ibid., 96–97.
8. Thomas Lynch, "What Shall We Say," *Christian Century*, June 7, 2015, https://www.christiancentury.org/artsculture /poems/what-shall-we-say. Reprinted by permission.

Chapter 3: The Black Glacier

1. Collins, "Aristotle," 101–2.
2. Seamus Heaney, "Clearances," in *Opened Ground: Selected Poems 1966–1996* (New York: Farrar, Straus and Giroux, 1998), 290.
3. Dennis O'Driscoll, *Stepping Stones: Interviews with Seamus Heaney* (New York: Farrar, Straus and Giroux, 2010), 473.
4. Ibid.
5. Seamus Heaney, "Funeral Rites," in *Poems, 1965–1975* (New York: Noonday Press, 1988), 170.
6. Seamus Heaney, "Miracle," in *Human Chain: Poems* (New York: Farrar, Straus, and Giroux, 2011), 16.
7. Thomas Lynch, "Refusing at Fifty-two to Write Sonnets," in *Walking Papers: Poems, 1999–2009* (New York: W. W. Norton, 2010), 85.

Chapter 4: Some Thoughts on Uteri, on Wombs

1. Robert G. Ingersoll, "At a Child's Grave," in *The Best of Robert Ingersoll*, ed. Roger E. Greeley (Amherst, NY: Prometheus Books, 1993), 111–12.

Chapter 5: Euclid and the Properties of Love and Eucharist (On Michael Heffernan)

1. Thomas Lynch, "Euclid," in *Walking Papers: Poems, 1999–2009* (New York: W. W. Norton, 2010), 11.
2. Michael Heffernan, "Geometric," in *At the Bureau of Divine Music* (Detroit: Wayne State University Press, 2011), 44.
3. Lynch, "Euclid," 11.
4. Michael Heffernan, "The Crazyman's Revival," in *The Cry of Oliver Hardy* (Athens, GA: University of Georgia Press, 1979), 27–28.

5. Thomas Lynch, "Michael's Reply to the White Man," in *Skating with Heather Grace* (New York: Knopf, 1986), 3.
6. Heffernan, "Geometric," 44–45.
7. Lynch, "Euclid."

Chapter 6: This Is Just to Say (On William Carlos Williams)

1. William Carlos Williams, "This Is Just to Say," in *The Collected Poems of William Carlos Williams, vol. 1, 1909–1939*, Christopher MacGowan, ed. (New York: New Directions, 1991), 372.
2. Williams, "The Young Housewife," in *The Collected Poems*, 57.
3. Williams, "Tract," in *The Collected Poems*, 72.
4. Ibid., 73–74.
5. Emily Dickinson, "After great pain, a formal feeling comes," in *The Complete Poems of Emily Dickinson*, Thomas H. Johnson, ed. (Boston: Back Bay Books, 1976), 3.
6. Williams, "The Red Wheelbarrow," in *The Collected Poems*, 224.
7. Thomas Lynch, "Refusing at Fifty-two to Write Sonnets," in *Walking Papers: Poems, 1999–2009* (New York: W. W. Norton, 2010), 85.

Chapter 7: Poets, Popes, and Laureates (On Carol Ann Duffy)

1. Carol Ann Duffy, "River," in *The World's Wife* (New York: Farrar, Straus, and Giroux, 2001), 68.
2. Ibid.
3. Duffy, "Pope Joan," in *The World's Wife*, 68–69.

Chapter 8: Haunts (On Michael Donaghy)

1. William Butler Yeats, "To Be Carved on a Stone at Thoor Ballylee," in *The Collected Poems of W. B. Yeats* (New York: Wordsworth Poetry Library, 1994), 162.
2. Michael Donaghy, "Reprimands," in *Collected Poems* (New York: Pan Macmillan, 2009), 139–40.
3. Donaghy, "Pentecost," in *Collected Poems*, 2.

4. Donaghy, "Reprimands," 21.
5. Donaghy, "Haunts," in *Collected Poems*, 46.

Chapter 11: On Asses

1. G. K. Chesterton, "The Donkey," in *The Collected Poems of G. K. Chesterton* (New York: Dodd, Mead & Company, 1932), 325.
2. Ibid.

Chapter 12: The Good Funeral and the Empty Tomb

1. Thomas Lynch, *The Undertaking: Life Studies from the Dismal Trade* (New York: W. W. Norton, 1997), 83–84.
2. Adapted with permission from *The Good Funeral: Death, Grief, and the Community of Care*, Thomas G. Long and Thomas Lynch (Louisville, KY: Westminster John Knox Press, 2013).
3. Zygmunt Bauman, *Morality, Immorality, and Other Life Strategies* (Stanford, CA: Stanford University Press, 1992), 51.
4. Thomas Long, *Accompany Them with Singing: The Christian Funeral* (Louisville, KY: Westminster John Knox Press, 2013), 73.

Chapter 13: The Sin-eater

1. Thomas Lynch, "The Sin-eater," in *The Sin-eater: A Breviary* (Brewster, MA: Paraclete Press, 2011), 3.
2. Robert Habenstein and William Lamers, *The History of American Funeral Directing* (Milwaukee: Bulfin, 1955), 128.

Chapter 15: Shilling Life

1. W. H. Auden, "Who's Who," in *A Book of the Sonnet: Poems and Criticism*, Martin Kallich et al., ed. (New York: Twane Publishers, 1973), 79.
2. Emily Dickinson, "I'm nobody! Who are you?" in *The Complete Poems of Emily Dickinson* (Boston: Little Brown, 1961), 288.

3. Ernest Dowson, "Envoy," in *Great Short Poems*, Paul Negri, ed. (Mineola, NY: Dover, 2000), 40.
4. Hilda Doolittle, "Lethe," in *Collected Poems, 1912–1944*, Louis L. Martz, ed. (New York: New Directions, 1986), 190.
5. James Joyce, "A Painful Case," in *Dubliners* (New York: Penguin, 1993), 43.

Chapter 16: Movable and Steadfast Feasts

1. Thomas Lynch, "Twelve Days of Christmas," *CYPHERS*, Dublin, CD commemorative issue, 2016. Reprinted by permission.
2. William Wordsworth, "Nuns Fret Not at Their Convent's Narrow Room," in *The Longman Anthology of Poetry*, Lynne McMahon and Averill Curdy, eds. (New York: Pearson/ Longman, 2006), https://www.poetryfoundation.org/ poems/52299/nuns-fret-not-at-their-convents-narrow-room.
3. Thomas Lynch, "Corpses Do Not Fret Their Coffin Boards," in *Walking Papers: Poems* (New York: W. W. Norton, 2010), 21.